SECOND EDITION

B2 VANTAGE
SUCCESS WITH
BUSINESS

SUCCESS WITH BUSINESS resources (including audio and answer sheets for the practice exam)

http://www.eltexampreparation.com/success/success-business

Password: succ!BUS#2

T0349585

**NATIONAL
GEOGRAPHIC
LEARNING**

Australia · Brazil · Mexico · Singapore · United Kingdom · United States

NATIONAL GEOGRAPHIC
LEARNING

National Geographic Learning,
a Cengage Company

Success with Business Vantage Workbook
Paul Dummett

Publisher: Sharon Jervis

Project Manager: Hattie Fell

Editorial Manager: Claire Merchant

Head of Strategic Marketing ELT: Charlotte Ellis

Product Marketing Manager ELT: Victoria Taylor

Head of Production and Design: Celia Jones

Senior Content Project Manager: Sue Povey

Manufacturing Manager: Eyvett Davis

Composition: emc design ltd

Cover Design: emc design ltd

Audio Producer: James Richardson

The publishers would like to dedicate the
Success with Business series to the memory of its
inspirational editor, David Riley.

For permission to use material from this text or product,
submit all requests online at **cengage.com/permissions**
Further permissions questions can be emailed to
permissionrequest@cengage.com

ISBN: 978-1-4737-7248-9

National Geographic Learning
Cheriton House, North Way
Andover, Hampshire, SP10 5BE
United Kingdom

Locate your local office at **international.cengage.com/region**

Visit National Geographic Learning online at **ELTNGL.com**
Visit our corporate website at **www.cengage.com**

Acknowledgments

Cover Image: Riccardo Meloni/EyeEm/Getty

PHOTOS: pp 5 © ChesiireCat/iStock/Thinkstock, 6 © g-stockstudio/iStock/Thinkstock, 11 © KatarzynaBialesiewicz/
iStock/Thinkstock, 17 © Siri Stafford/DigitalVision/Thinkstock, 20 (1) © Jupiterimages/BananaStock/Thinkstock,
20 (2) © ayo888/iStock/Thinkstock, 20 (3) © pimpic/iStock/Thinkstock, 20 (4) © DS011/iStock/Thinkstock,
20 (5) © Michael Blann/Photodisc/Thinkstock, 20 (6) © ablokhin/iStock/Thinkstock, 20 (7) © Daviles/iStock/
Thinkstock, 20 (8) © gpetric/iStock/Thinkstock, 26 © CHUYN/iStock/Thinkstock, 34 © iofoto/iStock/Thinkstock,
35 © JackF/iStock/Thinkstock, 45 (b) © Chesnot/Contributor/Getty Images News/Getty Images, 45 (t) © Mike Kemp/
Contributor/Corbis News/Getty Images, 45 (m) © Bloomberg/Contributor/Bloomberg/Getty Images,
47 © moodboard/moodboard/Thinkstock, 55 © georgeclerk/Gettyimages.

Printed in the United Kingdom by Ashford Colour Press Ltd
Print Number: 05   Print Year: 2024

Module 1

1.1	Ways of working	5
1.2	Making contacts	7
1.3	Speaking Test: Part One	9

Module 2

2.1	Company benefits	10
2.2	Presenting a company	12
2.3	Reading Test: Part One	14

Module 3

3.1	Starting a business	15
3.2	Leaving and taking messages	17
3.3	Listening Test: Part One	19

Module 4

4.1	Advertising	20
4.2	Delegating	22
4.3	Writing Test: Part One Reading Test: Part Five	24

Module 5

5.1	The workplace	25
5.2	Participating in a meeting	27
5.3	Speaking Test: Part Two	29

Module 6

6.1	Recruitment	30
6.2	Electronic communication	32
6.3	Reading Test: Part Two	34

Module 7

7.1	Job qualities	35
7.2	Selling	37
7.3	Reading Test: Part Four	39

Module 8

8.1	Training	40
8.2	Showing you're listening	42
8.3	Listening Test: Part Two	44

Module 9

9.1	Branding	45
9.2	Getting through	47
9.3	Writing Test: Part Two	49

Module 10

10.1	Management	50
10.2	Solving problems	52
10.3	Listening Test: Part Three	54

Module 11

11.1	Ethical economics	55
11.2	Discussing trends	57
11.3	Reading Test: Part Three	59

Module 12

12.1	Business law	60
12.2	Handling questions	62
12.3	Speaking Test: Part Three	64

| | Answer key | 65 |

1   **Write the opposite of each phrase.**

0 to start work: to finish work

1 regular, fixed hours: _____ hours

2 a temporary job: a _____ job

3 to work part-time: to work _____

4 an employer: an _____

5 a staff (salaried) photographer:

a _____ photographer

2   **Complete the journalist's description of her working life by writing the correct preposition in each space.**

I've been working as a freelance journalist
(0) for six years. Before that, I worked (1) _____
a big daily newspaper in the business section, but I
didn't have the freedom to write the stories I wanted
to. In fact, I'm someone who needs to work
(2) _____ her own – I really enjoy being my own
boss. I dislike being (3) _____ an office too, but
fortunately I get out a lot. My work takes me all
(4) _____ the world, investigating stories from Rio to
Riyadh, according (5) _____ what interests me at the
time. At the moment, I'm working (6) _____ a story
about Japanese inventors. There's an interesting team
of them who are employed (7) _____ a big
electronics firm, but instead of being in a research
lab, they work (8) _____ home. The company thinks
this will open their minds. I'm not quite so sure,
because they have to report (9) _____ their bosses
every day about what they've been doing!

The disadvantage of working for yourself is that you
never take enough time (10) _____. Actually, that
doesn't matter to me, because I get to travel and work
(11) _____ a lot of interesting people.

When I'm (12) _____ home I relax a bit more,
as well as writing and doing research for the next
project.

3   **Each of these sentences contains one grammatical mistake. Find the mistake and correct it.**

0 I'm glad I don't have to get up ~~on~~ 6 o'clock every
morning!   *at 6 o'clock*

1 I work a five-days week. _____

2 I've been working there since a couple of months.
_____

3 I often work few extra hours on Monday.
_____

4 I am not every day in the office.
_____

5 I miss to chat to my colleagues.
_____

Pronunciation

4   **Check that you can pronounce the underlined words correctly.**

0 A busy <u>office</u>   good <u>advice</u>
   /ɒfɪs/ as in 'miss' and /ədvaɪs/ as in 'nice'

1 hard <u>work</u>   a long <u>walk</u>

2 part of a <u>team</u>   part-<u>time</u>

3 parental <u>leave</u>   <u>live</u> near the office

4 one <u>child</u>   three <u>children</u>

5 a job <u>share</u>   an office <u>chair</u>

Present tenses

5 Life coaches are employed by some busy executives to give advice about how they can manage their working lives. Below are some examples of this advice. Put the verbs in brackets in the present perfect simple or present perfect continuous tense.

0 It's all about work-life balance. You *have been working* (work) too hard and not relaxing enough.

1 Just because you _____ (do) the same thing for years, it doesn't mean you have to go on doing it.

2 If you _____ (have) the same job for seven years, it's probably time for a change.

3 If you _____ (know) only success in your life, failure can be very difficult to deal with.

4 Being at the top can seem lonely. The reason is probably that you _____ (not / listen) to other people enough.

5 You _____ (worry) too much about little things – the things that are important are your health, your family and your happiness.

6 Business should be a pleasure. As far as I can tell, for you up to now it _____ (be) a chore.

7 You _____ (think) about your standard of living and not your quality of life.

8 To get to where you are now _____ (be) your ambition all your life. I'm not surprised you feel uncertain about what to do next.

6 Write one more piece of 'life coach advice' for someone who works long hours.

7 Complete each sentence in your own words using the present simple or present continuous tense.

0 I'm not a qualified engineer yet.
  I *am still training.*

1 When I arrive at work, I always _____
  _____

2 I rarely _____
  _____ after 7 o'clock.

3 I usually drive to work, but this week I _____
  _____

4 At lunchtime, I generally _____
  _____

5 My boss _____
  _____ at the moment.

6 After work I often _____
  _____

7 Please don't disturb me now. I _____
  _____

8 When I speak English I sometimes _____
  _____

8 Write how long you have been doing OR have done these things:

0 live at your current address
  I've been living in a flat in London for
  six months (OR since July).

1 study English
  _____
  _____

2 work in your current job
  _____
  _____

3 have your mobile phone
  _____
  _____

4 know what you want to do in life
  _____
  _____

5 do these exercises
  _____
  _____

1 Choose the correct word(s) to complete each statement.

0 It's a small company – there are only 15 of us – and I'm responsible *for* / *of* answering the phone and making appointments for the director.

1 I've been working at Dell Computers for two years. I *am specialised / specialise* in examining international contracts to make sure that they comply with the law.

2 I'm in charge *of / for* a small team of workers in the Jaguar car plant. We work on the engine assembly line.

3 Remploy is a company that employs disabled people. I *handle / deal* with the media and try to get us as much good publicity as possible.

4 I am quite independent and I *report / depend* directly to the Managing Director. I'm involved *in / by* making sure the company's activities have a positive impact on the environment.

5 I work *with / for* a specialist garage. We repair and restore old vintage models, like Rolls Royce and Bugatti.

2 Match each of the descriptions in exercise 1 to these job titles.

A Legal advisor

B Head of Sustainable Development

C Personal assistant = *O*

D Production foreman

E **Press officer**

F **Car mechanic**

3 Read the job advertisement and then answer the questions.

1 What will the HR officer be mainly responsible for?

2 What else does the job involve?

3 Who will he / she report to?

4 What will he / she need to attend from time to time?

5 What doesn't he / she have to have for this job?

Post: **HR Officer**
Organisation: **Green Associates**
Salary: £35,000 plus excellent benefits and progression

Are you looking to join a rapidly growing advertising agency in central London? Your duties are to recruit staff at all levels across the firm. Working directly under the HR manager, you will support her in all projects relating to Human Resource development of the organisation: recruitment, training and career development. You will also represent the company at conferences and job fairs. The successful candidate will have good organisational skills, experience of recruitment and the ability to work to tight deadlines. Previous knowledge of the sector is not necessary, as training will be given.

4 Correct the underlined phrases in this conversation between people meeting at a conference.

Barney Hello, Sara, good to see you again. Can I introduce you to Su Li?

Sara How are you do, Su Li? I'm Sara.
How do you do?

Su Li It's a pleasure. Please call me Su.

Sara I am pleased meeting you, too. Barney has told me about you. How long were you here?

_____

_____

Su Li I arrived in London two days ago.

Sara And is that your first time in England?

_____

Su Li Yes, it is.

Sara How you like?

_____

Su Li London is great, but rather expensive.

Sara Well, can I join to you two for a coffee?

_____

Su Li Yes, sure. Are you enjoying the conference?

Sara Yes, it has been very useful. I make a lot of new contacts. And you?

_____

Su Li Yes, it's new for me, but I have learnt a lot.

Sara You work for Taylor Associates, isn't it?

_____

Su Li Yes, I am their Chinese agent. And you are with Featherstone, I think.

Sara Yes, this is right.

_____

Correspondence

5 **Read the two emails and say which one definitely requires action. Write a short reply to the one that requires action.**

A

Hi David

Thanks for your message. I'm sorry to hear that you didn't get the job. To be honest, I expected them to give it to someone with more experience. You've only been working there for nine months. Anyway, how about a drink some time? Let me know when is good for you.

Kate

B

Dear Ms Kowlowski

I am writing to apologise for the mistake we made with your order. The correct item is now on its way and should be with you in the next couple of days. Do not hesitate to contact me if I can be of further assistance.

Kind regards

Alfonso Alvares

6 **Convert these short messages from an informal to a formal style using the words given.**

0 Please don't forget to call Kate. She wants your answer. (remind / contact / would like)
May I remind you to contact Kate. She would like to know your answer.

1 Just a quick note to say that we have got your order and it will be with you very soon.
(writing / inform / received / arrive shortly)

_____

_____

2 I am sorry for the mistake with the invoice. Here is the correct one.
(apologise / incorrect / attaching / version)

_____

_____

3 We met earlier in the week. I'm now sending you the information you asked for. (further / meeting / please / attach / requested)

_____

_____

7 **Convert these short messages from a formal to an informal style using the words given.**

0 Please find attached the estimate for the plumbing work. Please do not hesitate to contact me if you require further information.
(Here / estimate / plumbing / in touch / need / more)
Here is the estimate for the plumbing work. Please get in touch if you need any more information.

1 I am afraid I will be unable to attend the meeting this afternoon. I would be grateful if you could tell me the result.
(sorry / can't / please / let / know / happens)

_____

2 I would like to suggest that we meet at the restaurant. Unfortunately, I will only have an hour.
(how / meeting / ? / bad news)

_____

3 It was a pleasure to see you last week and I am looking forward to our next meeting.
(good / hope / again soon)

_____

8 **You are a salesperson for a lighting company. You want to visit some lighting shops in the UK next month to show your product range. Write an email of 40–50 words to the owners of these shops explaining when and why you would like to visit them. Use the framework below.**

Dear Mr _____

I represent _____

_____

I will be _____

_____

Please suggest _____

_____

I look _____

_____

Speaking Test: Part One

1 Fill in the missing words in each question to complete the dialogue from a speaking exam.

Examiner So, Paolo. (0) *Where* are you *from*?

Paolo My home town is near Milan in Italy.

Examiner And (1) _____ do you do?

Paolo I'm a student at a business college

Examiner (2) _____ _____ have you been studying?

Paolo Three years. I'm in my final year.

Examiner (3) _____ you have a job lined up afterwards?

Paolo Yes. I'm going to work for my father's company.

Examiner (4) _____ _____ _____ company is it?

Paolo We make jewellery.

Examiner And (5) _____ will your job _____?

Paolo I will be working in marketing, trying to develop international business.

Examiner And (6) _____ do you feel _____ working for your father?

Paolo Well, actually, he is semi-retired now, so we won't see a lot of each other.

2 Read the examiner's questions and say what you are being asked to talk about in each case.

company's activity	~~work duties~~
ambitions	your opinion	job prospects
hobbies	

0 What does your job involve? *work duties*

1 What do you do in your spare time?

2 What are your long-term goals?

3 What line of business are they in?

4 What do people on the course generally go on to do?

5 How do you feel about working abroad?

3 The responses of this candidate are a bit short! Expand each one into a full answer.

Examiner Where are you from?

Candidate Vienna. (0) *I'm Austrian. I come from Vienna originally.*

Examiner And are you working at the moment?

Candidate Yes, the last six months.

(1) _____

Examiner What do you do exactly?

Candidate Trainee, sales.

(2) _____

Examiner Can you tell me a bit about the company?

Candidate Cosmetics.

(3) _____

Examiner Who are your main customers?

Candidate Department stores, pharmacies.

(4) _____

Examiner Do you have to use English in your work?

Candidate Not yet.

(5) _____

Examiner What do you think about the testing of cosmetics on animals?

Candidate What? (6) _____

Examiner What do you think about the testing of cosmetics on animals?

Candidate It's terrible. (7) _____

Examiner And what would you like to do in the future?

Candidate International manager.

(8) _____

4 Now use the prompts below to write long answers to the questions in exercise 3. How do these compare with your own answers?

1 working / company / called / six months

2 moment / just / working / trainee / department

3 manufacture / sell / range / products

4 mainly / sell to

5 moment / hope / future

6 Sorry / repeat ?

7 know / people / disagree / I / really / problem / actually

8 ambition / manager / abroad

2.1   Company benefits

1 Complete this list of job benefits using the words in the box.

> unpaid   promotion   off   pension
> company   flexible   ~~good~~   holiday

Your employment package will include:

- a (0) *good* salary
- use of a (1) _____ car
- (2) _____ working hours
- excellent opportunities for (3) _____
- a full (4) _____ on retirement
- possibility of (5) _____ leave
- five weeks' annual (6) _____
- one day (7) _____ per month for personal training

2 Complete the expressions using *take*.

0 I am taking a *trip* to Madrid next week. I hope I'll get some time to see the city.

1 Don't worry. Andrew is an excellent host. He will take _____ of you.

2 We have taken _____ a temporary secretary for three months to help us get through the work.

3 I think we should take a _____. We've been discussing this for two hours now.

4 You should take what she says with a _____ of salt.

5 The conference will take _____ in New York in October next year.

3 Read the passage about job title inflation and choose the best sentence (A–G) to complete each gap (1–6).

A That's a lot of coaches and not very many players.

B Have you got greater responsibilities?

C They make a public statement that this employee is important to the company.

D In terms of the job they actually do, the title is meaningless.

E In other words, you are doing the same job, but it now has a grander title.

F After all, the company cannot be made up of only high-flying managers.

G The other will be to have an impressive job title.

Have you just been promoted to the status of manager? Then ask yourself these questions: Has your salary risen significantly? (0) B Have your benefits increased? If not, then you are probably the victim of what is known as 'job title inflation'. (1) _____

One in four company employees in London are now managers. (2) _____ It cannot be the case that companies need so many people giving orders and so few people taking them. So we can only conclude that these managers are managers in name only. (3) _____

So why do companies continue to hand out these titles? The answer is simple. They are a cheap way to recognise an employee's commitment to the job and to give them an incentive to stay. (4) _____ If you ask an MBA student these days what their ambitions are, one will certainly be to pick up a fat pay cheque some day. (5) _____

But companies have to be careful. Too many title promotions can lead to employees feeling suspicious about their value. (6) _____ If the company keeps creating new titles (Senior, Deputy, Vice-President, Marketing and so on) their significance soon decreases.

The past

4 Look at the underlined verbs in this dialogue. If the verb is in the correct tense, write 'correct'. If it is incorrect, write the correct form.

Interviewer So, I see from your CV that you are currently with Cadbury's. How long <u>did you work</u> (0) *have you been working* there?

Candidate I <u>have joined</u> (1) _____ them in 2014. At first, I <u>worked</u> (2) _____ in the sales department but more recently I <u>worked</u> (3) _____ in the Marketing Innovation department.

Interviewer That sounds interesting. What <u>have you done</u> (4) _____ there exactly?

Candidate We <u>have been researching</u> (5) _____ what products we should sell into our new markets in the Far East. In some cases we <u>took</u> (6) _____ an existing product and rebranded it. In other cases we <u>have been developing</u> (7) _____ a completely new product.

Interviewer And you <u>lived</u> (8) _____ in Australia until last January. Is that right?

Candidate Yes, we <u>have moved</u> (9) _____ back to the UK in February. I <u>have looked</u> (10) _____ for a new job since then.

5 Write the profile of this company using the facts in the box. Begin like this:

Reynard Inc is based in Birmingham in the UK. The company ...

Company name:	Reynard Inc
Headquarters:	Birmingham, UK
Established:	1906
Main products:	Bicycles and motorcycles
Experience:	Over 50 years motorcycle manufacture
Subsidiaries:	USA and Hungary (last year)
Recent developments:	New partnership with Chinese factory

Pronunciation

6 Look at this extract from a presentation and mark where you think the natural pauses should go.

```
I think we all recognise that
incentives are important, but why? And
what kind of incentives work best?
Should they be financial or should we
concentrate on praising employees for
good work or for achieving their
targets? The answer is not simple
because not every individual responds
in the same way.
```

7 The letter 'i' can be pronounced /aɪ/ as in *nice,* or /ɪ/ as in *quick.* Sort the words from the box into the correct column in the table.

recognise incentive promise finance
individual outline policy final flexible
benefit behind article division describe

Long 'i' /aɪ/	Short 'i' /ɪ/
recognise	

2.2 Presenting a company

1 Complete the company profile of a French energy company, by choosing the correct word A–D below to fill each gap.

HOME | INVESTING | NEWS & OPINION | PERSONAL FINANCE

TOP STORIES As of 5 minutes ago

EDF is one of the largest electricity companies in the world with a (0) B of 75 billion Euros in 2016.

Its (1) _____ are in Paris, and it is the dominant player in France, with over 80% of the market.

Its largest (2) _____ , 100% owned by EDF, is EDF-Energy which supplies over five million customers in the UK.

The company has three main (3) _____: electricity production, of which 70% comes from nuclear power (4) _____ ; distribution; and retail or supply. The first two are very technical activities. The third, retail, is more customer focused. Nowadays, most customer contact is handled by (5) _____ centres, where operators manage customer enquiries online or over the telephone.

Electricity is an unusual product. It cannot be stored in a (6) _____ like other goods. What you produce has to be consumed immediately. So, supply and demand have to be balanced exactly on a day by day, or hour by hour basis.

0	A sales	B	turnover
	C income	D	figure
1	A base	B	foundation
	C headquarters	D	seat
2	A subsidiary	B	subsidy
	C substation	D	daughter
3	A agencies	B	corporations
	C holdings	D	divisions
4	A factories	B	plants
	C branches	D	centres
5	A call	B	phone
	C ring	D	telecoms
6	A depot	B	holding
	C plant	D	warehouse

2 Write these numbers in words (as you would say them).

0 542 *five hundred and forty-two*

1	60%	2	1905 (the year)
3	2008 (the year)	4	5,000,000
5	3,210	6	½
7	$^{11}/_4$	8	33.3%

3 Put one word in each space to complete this extract from a presentation.

Thanks everyone (0) *for* coming. Today, I'd like to (1) _____ you a bit about our new company. I'll be (2) _____, so if you have any questions please wait and I'll be (3) _____ to answer them at the end.

First of (4) _____, how did we get the idea for Mobile Media? I met Steve, my partner, three months ago when he was working with Vodafone to …

One other thing I'd like to point (5) _____ is that this is not a technology just for the future. It is already being used in China and Korea.

… Finally, I'd just like to (6) _____ you this chart which (7) _____ an overview of all the possibilities that this technology offers. We are really excited about the prospects for it and I hope I've been able to communicate some of that enthusiasm to you today. Thanks for (8) _____. Are there any questions?

---

4 What comes next? Continue these presentation phrases using the prompts in brackets.

0 Thank you (come / today) *for coming today.*

1 I'd like to begin by (tell / something / product)

_____

2 At this point I will quote our CEO: (great / product / not enough) _____

_____

3 Let's move on (look / sales) _____

_____

4 This chart (show / turnover / 2017) _____

_____

5 Let's take a look (profits / last year) _____

_____

6 That brings me (end / presentation) _____

_____

Memos

5 Read the following memo and answer the questions.

1 What is the relationship between John Simmons and Graham Pole?

2 What is the problem?

3 What solution is proposed?

4 What action should Graham take next?

INTERNAL MEMO

To: Graham Pole

From: John Simmons

Date: 16 March

Subject: Absence from work

You have been absent from work for 22 days this year. I am aware that some of this was due to sickness, but if there is some other problem, you are welcome to come and chat to me any time. If I don't hear from you, I will expect your attendance to return to normal.

6 There are eight more mistakes in this memo. Find them and correct them.

INTERNAL MEMO

To: ~~Every~~ All staff

From: Sarah Kandarthi

Date: 9th of October

Subject: Suggestions for staff party

Just a quickly reminder that the staff party will be at 5 December. We have not done a final decision on where it will take place, so please to send me your suggestions. If anyone is not able attending, please make me know before the next Friday.

7 Read these two memos and replace the underlined phrases with the synonyms in the box.

| for further information   ~~as you may know~~ |
| I'd like to point out   further to   as a result |
| if you would like   because of   you hear from me |

INTERNAL MEMO

To: All sales staff

From: Davis Allan, Sales Director

Date: 12 February

Subject: Product defect – B3050

(0) <u>As you are probably aware,</u> As you may know a number of vacuum cleaners (Model B3050) have been returned with a faulty electrical connection. (1) <u>Consequently,</u> we are temporarily withdrawing this product from our list. Please do not try to sell any until (2) <u>further notice</u>. (3) <u>If you have any questions,</u> please contact me directly.

INTERNAL MEMO

To: All staff

From: Katja Ebert, Production Manager

Date: 7 May

Subject: Closure of Mannheim plant

(4) <u>Following</u> a meeting of the board on 6 May, the company has decided to close the plant in Mannheim. This is (5) <u>due to</u> recent poor results. There will be an official meeting to discuss the closure on 3 June. (6) <u>For anyone wishing</u> to attend, (7) <u>please note</u> that the deadline for registration is 21 May.

2.3 Reading Test: Part One

Exam Tip

Although in this type of matching exercise most of the statements refer to details in the text, it is very important to have a sense of the main idea being presented in each paragraph.

1 Read this paragraph and then choose the statement that best summarises it.

> The boom in demand for new home entertainment technology, such as flat-screen televisions and computers, is taking up worrying amounts of energy. The consumer electronics sector is now not far from being responsible for using more domestic electricity than any other source – more than lighting or kitchen appliances, for example. By 2020 it will account for 45 per cent of all electricity used in UK homes, cancelling out all other efforts to reduce energy use and fight climate change.

A   Demand in the electronics sector is particularly strong for home entertainment systems.

B   Demand for consumer electronics means we are using more energy when we should be trying to use less.

C   The amount of electricity used by kitchen appliances is growing.

2 Study the article below and write one sentence to summarise each paragraph.

Mood Foods

A   It is every marketer's dream. To take a product which people like, but feel they shouldn't consume too much of, and to present it as something which is beneficial to your health. 'Mental Balance Chocolate Gaba' is one such product; chocolate which actually does you good. Research has shown that Gaba, an acid naturally found in chocolate, can reduce anxiety and help people to feel less stressed. It is already on sale in Japan and demand is growing rapidly.

B   Gaba is just one in a family of products called 'mood foods' which are currently being promoted by the food industry. In the UK, sales of healthy or lifestyle foods are worth over £1 billion a year. In the past, however, companies have promoted the physical benefits of certain ingredients: such as strengthening your bones or reducing the risk of cancer. With this new range, the focus is much more on food that will help you to change your mood or emotional state.

C   Omega-3 is another example. It is claimed that it both boosts mental development and promotes good behaviour. It's no wonder that parents are trying to get it into their children as fast as possible. Traditionally, it has been found in dairy products, like milk and yoghurt, but marketers saw the opportunity to satisfy both parents' and children's requirements and now it can be found in cakes and sweets, too.

D   The success of these products has prompted companies to look for similar products, but food experts say we need to be a little cautious. 'The problem is,' says Dr Campbell of the Food Advice Bureau, 'people feel that by occasionally consuming one or two of these products, they can reap all the benefits. What they don't realise – and what the companies don't bother to tell them – is that everything that you eat is important.'

3 Now answer the exam question.

> • Look at the statements below and the article on 'Mood Foods' above.
> • Which paragraph (A, B, C or D) does each statement refer to? (You will need to use some of the letters more than once.)
>
> 1 Companies don't try to educate people about their whole diet. _____
> 2 A product that seems to be good for you and is also nice to eat is very easy to sell. _____
> 3 These new foods emphasise mental rather than physical effects. _____
> 4 Its benefits are to make you feel less worried. _____
> 5 Specialists think people should be careful about the advantages of eating specific products. _____
> 6 Its benefits are that it stimulates your mind. _____
> 7 People spend a lot of money on foods that are good for them. _____

3.1 Starting a business

1 Complete the crossword with words describing types of businesses.

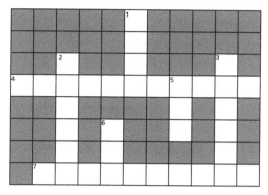

1 and 2 someone who runs a business alone
(4 and 6)

3 to be responsible for any financial losses (6)

4 a business where two or more individuals share the risk (11)

5 a phrasal verb meaning to establish: '_____ up' (3)

6 you do something by yourself or 'on your _____' (3)

7 businesses which have a licence to trade under another business name and following their business model (10)

2 Match each idiom or phrasal verb with the correct definition.

0 set up	A diversify into something new
1 upside	B the negative part of a situation
2 go it alone	C a new business that has just started
3 downside	D set up a business without help
4 start-up	E establish
5 branch out	F the positive part of a situation

3 Complete the text about the qualities of an entrepreneur by putting one of the words below into each gap.

> risks enthusiastic hard tested growth run
> ~~entrepreneurs~~ fail profit capital sense

Do you have what it takes to be an entrepreneur?

The most dynamic societies in the world are the ones that have the most (0) *entrepreneurs*. These people are the spark in an economy's engine, activating and stimulating economic (1) _____.

The entrepreneur looks for opportunities to make a (2) _____ by satisfying unsatisfied needs, to fill the gap between what consumers want and the products and services that are currently available.

Do you fit the description of an entrepreneur?

- Entrepreneurs are creative, (3) _____ and future oriented.

- They are innovators who don't need to follow the tried and (4) _____ route.

- They have a natural business (5) _____.

- They are not afraid of (6) _____ work or afraid to (7) _____.

- They are willing to take (8) _____ with their own (9) _____ and resources.

- They are excellent problem solvers and negotiate the legal requirements to launch and (10) _____ a business.

- They focus on sales, cash flow and revenue at all times.

will and the future

4 Study the different future forms in the table. Then choose the form that would best complete the sentences below.

Present simple	A timetabled or scheduled event
Present continuous	Something that has been firmly arranged
will (1)	A prediction about the future
will (2)	A promise of action or an offer
going to + infinitive	A plan or intention (already decided)
Future continuous	A continuous action in the future
Future perfect	A completed action in the future

0 This time tomorrow I ... + Future continuous

1 ... at 11am, followed by lunch at 1pm. _____

2 I've decided that I ... _____

3 By the end of the year we ... _____

4 If you like, I ... _____

5 I think that she ... _____

6 ... in the pub at 6 o'clock. _____

5 Match each phrase below to one of the phrases in exercise 4 to make a correct sentence.

0 If you like I'll pick you up from the station.

1 _____ will have sold over one million units.

2 _____ will be lying on a beach in Bermuda. I can't wait!

3 I'm meeting her _____.

4 The seminar takes place _____

5 _____ will probably get the job.

6 _____ am going to set up my own consultancy business.

6 Complete each short dialogue using the most appropriate future form.

0 **A** Have you seen my mobile phone anywhere?
  B No, I haven't. But I'll *keep* (keep) my eyes open.

1 **A** Would you like to go for a drink this evening?
  B I'm sorry, I can't. I _____ (have) dinner with some clients.

2 **A** Can I call you with an answer tomorrow – around 10?
  B No. I _____ (drive) up to Leeds then. Call me after 12.

3 **A** Have you decided how to break the bad news to her?
  B Yes, I _____ (tell) her directly. I think that's the only way.

4 **A** So, what's the programme for tomorrow?
  B Well, our train _____ (leave) at 9.15, so I think we _____ (get) some breakfast and go.

5 **A** What do you think our chances of success are?
  B I am fairly confident we _____ (win) the contract, but I also think they _____ (try) to get a better price from us.

6 **A** When can you let me have your report?
  B I _____ (finish) it by next Thursday, at the latest.

7 **A** I'm really having trouble loading this programme.
  B Here, I _____ (help) you. I'm good with computers.

8 **A** Do you have any plans for the weekend?
  B Well, I _____ (play) golf with Lee tomorrow and on Sunday I _____ (relax) with the family.

3.2 Leaving and taking messages

Leaving messages

1 Write in words how you would say the following.

0 25 June *the twenty-fifth of June*

1 14 May 2009

_____

2 2–5pm

_____

3 0778 322 1010

_____

4 JG13X

_____

5 O -'-R-E- I-L-L-Y

_____

6 www.yell.com

_____

7 karen@gmail.fr

_____

2 Complete the phrases by adding one word. The first letter has been given for you.

0 Please call me back.

1 Sachiko is trying to get h_____ of you.

2 I'm just r_____ your call.

3 Let me r_____ that back to you.

4 I'll call you b_____ in an hour.

5 You can g_____ me on this number any time.

6 The r_____ I'm calling is that …

3 Match each of these phrases with the one closest in meaning in exercise 2.

A I'm phoning with regard to …

B I can always be reached on my mobile.

C I'd be grateful if you could return my call. *O*

D She needs to speak to you.

E Can I just check that I wrote that down correctly?

F You phoned earlier.

G I will phone you again in an hour.

4 Complete the dialogue using one word in each gap.

Sanja Hello, Jurevic Investments.

Jose Hello, (0) this is Jose Moya from SRL in Madrid. Can I speak (1) _____ Mico, please?

Sanja I'm sorry, Mr Moya, Mr Jurevic is (2) _____ of the office today. Can I help you?

Jose Well, it's with (3) _____ to my diary. I met Mr Jurevic yesterday and I think (4) _____ mistake I picked up his diary and he picked up mine. Did he mention it to you?

Sanja Oh dear. No, he didn't say anything. But perhaps I can call him now and get him to call you (5) _____.

Jose I would be very (6) _____.

Sanja Is there a number I can (7) _____ you on, if I can't get through to him?

Jose Yes, you can get me any time (8) _____ my mobile. It's 06966 39941, but I'll be in the office all day today.

Sanja I'll just (9) _____ that back to you. It's 06966 39941.

Jose Yes, that's right. Thank you (10) _____ your help. Goodbye.

5 Complete the message form using the information in the dialogue.

Message for: _____

From: _____

Subject: _____

Action needed: _____

Contact details: _____

Taking notes and messages

6 When you arrive at work in the morning, you find the following four recorded messages on the answerphone. Read the transcripts of the messages and complete the notes. Use one word per space.

A

> Hello. Is anyone there … no? … OK, this is Aran from Bangkok House Restaurant. Ms Gerhard asked us on Friday for a price for a set dinner for 30 people. I have prepared a possible menu and the price. Can you ask her to call me on 0208 733 4545?

Message for: Ms Gerhard

Message from: _____ at _____ _____ _____

Subject: He has _____ _____ and _____ for set dinner

Action: Please call him _____ _____

B

> Hello, I'm trying to contact Mr Sato. My name is John Davies. It's quite urgent actually, but a little confidential. I'd be grateful if he could return my call as soon as possible. He knows the number.

Message for: Mr Sato

Message from: _____ _____

Subject: _____

Action: Please _____ _____ as soon as possible.

C

> Hello, this is Terry Jones from Guest Office Supplies. I think you were interested in our offer on office chairs – item G604 in our catalogue. I'm just calling to say that the offer ends this week, so if you would like to place an order, please contact me soon.

Message from: Terry Jones

Subject: Please note that the _____ on _____ _____ ends _____ _____

Action: Let _____ _____ soon if we are interested.

D

> Hello, this is a message for Sarah Jenas. We had an appointment for 4.30 on Friday but unfortunately I missed it. I'm very sorry. I would like to arrange another time this week. Would Thursday afternoon be possible? Please can she call to say if she is available then? Oh, sorry, I forgot to give my name – it's Maria Sanchez.

Message for: Sarah Jenas

Message from: _____ _____

Subject: She apologised for _____ the _____ _____ Friday. Would like to _____ _____ Thursday afternoon.

Action: Please call to _____

Pronunciation

7 Match each letter to the correct vowel sound and complete the table.

A E G H I J O Q R T U W Y Z

/eɪ/	/iː/	/aɪ/	/əʊ/	/ɑː/	/uː/	/e/
A		I				
					U	
	T					

8 Write the names as they are spelt out below.

0 diː – eɪ – viː – aɪ – iː – es   Davies

1 dʒeɪ – eɪ – dʒɜː – dʒɜː – iː – ɑː

2 es – tiː – aɪ – piː – iː

3 siː – əʊ – biː – eɪ – aɪ – en

Listening Test: Part One

1 Look at these notes to fill in from Part One of the Listening Test and try to predict what will go in each space. Write your predictions using one or two words.

A

Changes to conference

Date: (1) _____

Venue: (2) _____

3–4pm session: Speaker cancelled

New speaker: (3) _____

Title: (4) _____

B

Customer Services – Messages

Caller's name: Jackie Brown

Company: (5) _____ Limited

Item Ordered: (6) _____

Problem: Incorrect invoice. We (7) _____ the customer.

Action: Credit (8) £ _____ to her account.

C

Reminder of Training Session

Date: 4 July

Course Title: (9) _____

Participants: (10) _____

Venue: Galaxy Hotel

To reserve a place: Send back (11) _____ to Lisa Melrose in HR.

D

HR department – Messages

Caller's name: Buddy Richards

Subject: Job interview

Problem: He has an interview on (12) _____ but he is unable to attend because he is (13) _____ . He is very (14) _____ the job. Is it possible for us to give him a (15) _____ ?

2 Now study the transcripts and write the correct answers for exercise 1.

A

A Hi, I'm calling about the IT conference on the 3 May.

B Do you mean the one at the National Institute? Is there a problem?

A Well, yes and no. The speaker for the 3 o'clock session has just cancelled.

B Oh, dear, that was Laura Dean, wasn't it? She's really good. I've heard her speak before.

A Yes, I know, it's a pity. Luckily, Steve Johnson here in our office has volunteered to speak in her place.

B Steve Johnson? Has he? What is he going to talk about?

A He has done a lot of work on new mobile phone technology, so he is proposing 'Mobile Future' as the name for his session.

B OK, that sounds good. I'll change the conference programme.

B

A Hello, can I speak to someone in Customer Services, please?

B Yes, you're through to Customer Services. My name is Kieran Donahue. How can I help you?

A My name is Jackie Brown. I'm calling from Global Media Limited. We ordered a leather sofa from you last week.

B Has it not arrived yet?

A Yes, it has arrived, and it's very nice, thank you. That's not the problem. The problem is that on the invoice you sent, you have overcharged us.

B One moment. You bought the Chesterfield leather sofa at £1,500.

A That's right, but the invoice is for £1,800.

B That's obviously a mistake. I will get the difference of £300 credited to your account.

A Thanks. I'd appreciate that.

C

A You have reached the voicemail of Kerry Hirsch. I'm sorry I'm not here to take your call. Please leave a message and I'll call you back. BEEEEP

B Hello, Kerry, this is Lisa Melrose from HR. Just a reminder that the training course entitled 'Buying signals' will take place on the 4th July at the Galaxy Hotel. All the sales managers, both from here and abroad, are being invited to participate. It's not compulsory, but I think it will be a really useful day. If you are interested, can you send back the registration form that I emailed to you by Friday at the latest? Thanks.

D

A Hello, Birgit Henseler speaking.

B Oh, hello, my name is Buddy Richards. I applied for the job as a recruitment officer.

A Yes, I remember. You have an interview next week. How can I help?

B Well, that's the problem really. You asked me to come at 10am on 10 July, but I'm actually on holiday that week.

A Oh, that is difficult, because it's a group interview.

B Oh, I didn't realise that. I am very keen on the job. It sounds perfect for me. I was wondering if you could give me a telephone interview instead.

A I'm sorry, we do insist on meeting all candidates. Is there no possibility you could change your holiday dates?

4.1   Advertising

1   Match the photographs with the advertising terms.

TV commercial   mailshot   banner   spam
word of mouth   sample   billboard   loyalty card

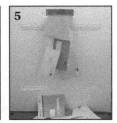

2   Complete the article by putting one preposition in each gap.

Advertising complaints

- 271 people reported a tax office advertisement (0) *to* the ASA (Advertising Standards Authority). It showed a plumber hiding under the kitchen sink to avoid paying his taxes. They objected (1) _____ the fact that it suggested that self-employed people were dishonest.

- 145 people complained (2) _____ a mobile phone advertisement that gave the idea that its service was 'free forever'.

- 99 complaints were received about an advertisement (3) _____ a TV programme called 'Nothing good ever came out of America'. The programme makers responded (4) _____ the complaints by saying that the programme was, in fact, promoting American culture (5) _____ viewers.

- A TV commercial advertising breakfast cereal (6) _____ children featured a man riding a dog. 96 people complained that children looking (7) _____ the image would try to do the same thing (8) _____ home.

3   Read the text about viral marketing (advertising messages that are spread by the users themselves) and put the sentences A–E into the correct place.

The ALS ice bucket challenge

A classic example of viral marketing was the ice bucket challenge taken up by people around the world to raise awareness and funds for research for the ALS disease (amyotrophic lateral sclerosis). (0) *C*

- Someone was nominated by a friend to take the challenge. Once they accepted, they had 24 hours to carry out the challenge.
- The idea was that the person challenged would have a bucket of ice cold water poured over their head. (1) _____
- When someone took the challenge, they were filmed. (2) _____
- The videos spread and soon everyone was doing the challenge. (3) _____
- Eventually the videos were everywhere and hundreds of people were taking up the challenge. Many people even took the challenge and made a donation.
- (4) _____ But as well as raising money, the campaign raised public awareness of the disease.

A Next, the video went on YouTube™ and on social media.

B If they didn't do it, they made a donation for ALS.

C The strategy was clever and very simple.

D In the end, $115 million was raised through the ice bucket challenge.

E In the case of famous celebrities, the videos appeared on TV.

4   Here are some opinions about the advantages and disadvantages of viral marketing. Replace each phrase in bold with one of the phrases below.

suppose   relatively   ~~tend to~~
on the other hand   remember   not sure

0 People **generally** respond to viral advertisements if they make them laugh. *tend to*

1 I **imagine** that it's successful because it's similar to word-of-mouth advertising.

2 I am **uncertain** about the ethics of it. Is it legal?

3 Viral ads can reach a lot of people. **But,** the response is not always positive.

4 I think it's great: it's new, **quite** cheap and has more impact than TV commercials.

5 **Don't forget** that 'viral' is a very negative word. It suggests you need to be protected from it.

Modals

5 Read these advertising guidelines and put the most appropriate modal verb into each gap. Use *must, mustn't, should, shouldn't* or *don't have to.*

0 Advertisers of alcoholic drinks mustn't advertise to children.

1 Advertisers of alcoholic drinks _____ make advertisements which could appeal to children.

2 When advertising a product, you _____ mention the price.

3 When advertising a product, you _____ make false statements about competitors' products.

4 If you advertise a service, you _____ explain the full terms and conditions, except in the small print.

5 Advertisers of medicines _____ be truthful about their benefits.

6 Advertisers of cosmetics products _____ try to be as truthful as possible about their benefits.

6 Put the most appropriate modal verb into each gap. Use *must, must have, can't* or *can't have.*

0 It must be difficult to advertise your service, because it's very complicated.

1 His report is only two pages long. It _____ taken him much time to write it.

2 There's no answer from her phone. She _____ switched it off.

3 There _____ be some other way to contact her. Try calling the New York office.

4 The advertisement doesn't mention the special offer. They _____ read my brief properly.

5 He _____ be changing job. He's only been there a month.

6 There _____ be some mistake. I definitely reserved a double room.

7 Read the dialogue between an advertising manager and a legal advisor. Then answer the questions.

1 What is the subject of the advertisement?

2 Is it possible to use the advertisement in its current form?

3 Did they make any changes before?

4 What option did they not choose when designing the advertisement?

Manager So, I understand that we can't now use this advertisement. What is the objection to it exactly?

Advisor They are not saying that you can't – just that changes will have to be made.

Manager I thought we had already improved it.

Advisor Actually, you needn't have changed the wording – that wasn't the problem.

Manager What was the problem?

Advisor The ASA are worried that the image could upset some people.

Manager It's supposed to be shocking. We could have made it more pleasant to look at, but people need to know that AIDS is a serious problem.

8 For each situation say what the person *should do / ought to do* or *should have done / ought to have done.* Use the words given to help you.

0 He invested all his money in Telecom shares and lost it in the stock market crash. (more carefully) He should have / ought to have invested his money more carefully.

1 They made the advertisement themselves and people said it looked cheap and unprofessional. (an advertising agency)

2 They have sent out over 10,000 letters in a mailshot but had very little response. (a different type of advertising)

3 They need to find a new receptionist. (the local paper)

4 They are losing customers to other supermarkets. (loyalty card)

5 He lost a lot of important data when a virus infected his computer. (anti-virus programme)

4.2 Delegating

1 Read the article 'Learning to let go for small businesses'. Write the correct heading for each paragraph.

A Growing into new roles

B Don't be afraid to bring in expertise

C ~~Growing a business~~

D Planning for the future

E Time to accept change

• • •

Learning to let go for small businesses

0 *C Growing a business*

It's a big challenge to start a business from nothing. You put all your effort into creating a new and original product or service. You start marketing and building relationships with customers. And as you grow you need to recruit more and more staff. This is a classic route for small sole trader companies and family firms.

1 _____

Obviously, fast growth for a small business is what everyone dreams of but it also comes with new challenges. One of the biggest challenges is decision making and learning that you can no longer be in charge of everything. It's hard to accept that you can't be everywhere and do everything, and to accept that some people may be better placed to do a job than you.

2 _____

You'll need to learn how to delegate and not to micromanage your subordinates. Of course, before you start delegating, you'll need to employ people whom you believe to be able to do the job. If you start delegating work to existing staff, you will need to give everyone time to get used to their new roles and new ways of doing things.

3 _____

If the transition to a more 'hands-off' approach proves difficult, it might be time to bring in an outside consultant to observe the process and give feedback or even run some in-house training. Again, small businesses sometimes find it difficult to bring in an outsider, but independent viewpoints and advice can be invaluable.

4 _____

Once you learn to let go, you'll find that it really takes the pressure off you and provides more time for long-term strategic planning. In return, your staff will enjoy the challenge of handling new responsibilities. It's also a good time to assess which staff are capable of moving into managerial positions as the company continues to grow.

2 Complete these delegating instructions by putting one word in each gap. The first letter has been given for you.

0 Please check the details in this conference programme and make any changes you think are necessary.

1 Can you give this email p_____ because the client wants an answer today?

2 Before you visit her, I need to b_____ you on the background to our dealings with her.

3 Feel f_____ to ask me if something is not clear.

4 You'll need to e_____ that all prices and other facts are correct before sending it out.

5 I'd like you to give me regular u_____ on your progress.

6 I think we should just go t_____ the main aims of the report before you start work on it.

7 Please remember that the d_____ for this offer is next Friday.

8 I'm going to put you in c_____ of the management of this project.

Pronunciation

3 Underline the three or four words in each sentence that are stressed the most.

0 I'd <u>like</u> <u>you</u> to be in <u>charge</u> of the <u>project</u>.

1 Please give priority to the Johnson case.

2 Let me know your answer by Tuesday.

3 You've done a great job on this!

4 One thing that's worrying me is the cost.

5 Can I borrow your computer for a moment?

6 I want you to go to Geneva.

7 When is the deadline for registration?

8 The main findings of the report were positive.

4 Check your answers to exercise 3 in the answer key, then practise saying the sentences, emphasising the stressed words and taking the stress off the others.

Reports

5 Match each phrase on the left with the one closest in meaning on the right.

0 The aim of this report is to …	A This means that …
1 As a result of this …	B The findings were that …
2 In conclusion …	C In the light of these results, I propose that we should …
3 It was found that …	D As well as …
4 Alternatively, we could …	E The purpose of this report is to …
5 The findings show that we ought to …	F To sum up …
6 In addition to …	G Another possibility would be to …

6 Put one of the phrases A–G from exercise 5 into each gap in the following report about the business strategy for a hotel.

To: The executive board

Re: Business strategy

(0) E describe the business strategy of a competitor, Bracken Hotels, and suggest what we can learn from them.

After visits to two different Bracken Hotels, (1) _____ their strategy is to target the business customer by offering the following services:

- secure parking and a car valeting service
- 24-hour room service and laundry service
- meeting rooms

(2) _____ this, they do not charge for cancellation if you tell them before 6 o'clock on the night you are going to stay. (3) _____ they are very busy during the week, but tend to be quieter at weekends.

(4) _____ offer similar services during the week and mail out a leaflet to companies advertising these. For meeting rooms, we could convert some existing bedrooms.

(5) _____ rent rooms in a nearby building.

(6) _____ , it seems that Bracken Hotels have a winning strategy for weekday guests and it would be a good idea to copy this.

---

7 Read the information and use the framework below to write a report.

You work in the marketing department of a company selling office supplies. The results of recent advertising campaigns have not been so good. Write a report to the executive board to explain this and what you propose to do about it. Use the information and notes below.

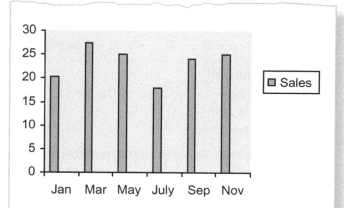

Marketing actions

Late February – mailout of special offers catalogue
best results here – suggest more of this

June – TV advertising
poor response and expensive

September – newspaper advertising campaign
response better but also expensive

November – mailout of new catalogue
not bad
Other possibilities – Internet advertising?

To:

Re:

Introduction and aims

Findings: Effect of advertising on sales

Conclusions

Recommendations

4.3 Writing Test: Part One
Reading Test: Part Five

Writing Test: Part One

1 Memos in the exam are supposed to be 40–50 words long. Look at the question and the candidate's answer, which is too long (100 words). Underline the most important information in the memo and cross out any phrases which give unnecessary detail. Then, write a shorter version of the memo.

> You work in the Human Resources department. The government has recently increased the amount of social security tax for all workers. Write a memo to your staff informing them:
> - what the change in tax is
> - who will be affected
> - when the new rules will take effect.
>
> | To: | All staff |
> |---|---|
> | From: | Daniel de Rivaz, Payroll Officer |
> | Date: | 13 May |
> | Subject: | Tax changes |
>
> I would like to point out to all staff that following the recent changes in the tax law announced by the government last week, in future the rate of social security tax will be 11%, which is an increase from the 10% it was before. This new rate will apply to everyone (the level of your salary is not important) and you will be taxed this amount starting in July. If you have any questions or want more information, you are welcome to contact me, Daniel de Rivaz, in the Human Resources department during normal office hours.

Reading Test: Part Five

2 Find the extra word in each sentence. Explain why it is wrong.

0 The company ~~don't~~ cannot know what motivates each employee the most.

You do not need two auxiliary verbs ('do' and 'can') and 'company' is a singular noun so 'don't' is incorrect.

1 For most people, it is more better to have an interesting job than a high salary.

2 The company encourages a people to go on training courses.

3 It is a job with a lot of variety and which with flexible working hours.

4 When you join to the company, you become part of a family.

5 But it is not only the company's responsibility. Each employee that has to motivate himself.

3 Answer the exam question.

> - Read the article with advice about language and workplace motivation.
> - In most of the lines there is one extra word. It is either grammatically incorrect or does not fit in with the sense of the text. Some lines are correct.
> - If a line is correct, write CORRECT next to the line. If there is an extra word, write it in CAPITALS next to the line.
>
> | 0 | When people talk about ways of motivating people at work, they naturally think of | CORRECT |
> |---|---|---|
> | 00 | pay increases or bonuses. But plenty of research that indicates that money is not the | THAT |
> | 1 | only motivator. In fact, once an employee earns at a certain level of salary, there are | _____ |
> | 2 | plenty of other factors which affect if how we respond to the workplace. Perhaps | _____ |
> | 3 | one of the most effective ways a manager can get to the best from his or her staff | _____ |
> | 4 | is through like using the right kind of language. A little bit of praise often goes a long | _____ |
> | 5 | way in improving morale and so does a simple 'thank you' from time to time. | _____ |
> | 6 | Simply showing interest in an employee's life also makes improves productivity. | _____ |
> | 7 | Managers who ask about someone's weekend or you show concern when a family | _____ |
> | 8 | member is ill naturally tend to receive similar consideration and support in return. | _____ |

1 Rearrange the words to make questions about buying art for a company.

0 how / companies / justify / do / the expense / ?
How do companies justify the expense?

1 what / tend / companies / do / kind / to buy / of art / ?

2 how / a company / ever / does / what art / agree on / to buy / ?

3 why / so / companies / do / choose / to buy / many / art / ?

4 who / if / I / should / want / a piece of art / consult / I / to buy / ?

5 does / matter / where / is displayed / the art / it / ?

6 commission / can / a work of art / to emphasise / you / your brand / ?

2 Complete the article about project management by choosing the best word to fill each gap.

Successful project management

The same project management rules can apply to all projects, whether the project is to commission a work of art, to construct new offices or to put in a new computer system. The (**0**) *based /* (basic) principles are these:

Understand the (1) *aims / ends* For example, the short-term objective of the project may be to install a computer system, but what is the long-term goal? It is this (2) *finish / end* result that you must focus on.

Decide who has ownership The person in the company who has (3) *commissioned / ordered* the project is the owner. It may be a specific department or a person, for example, the CEO. They are the customer in this case and the project (4) *manager / management* serves them.

Define the (5) *range / scope* This means the quantity of the project (how (6) *many / much* you want to achieve) and the quality (how good you need it to be).

Work out what resources you need This means not only the time and money you will have to (7) *expend / spend*, but also the (8) *specialist / special* knowledge you will need. Ensure you have enough of both to (9) *run / cope*.

Appoint a project manager A project manager has to (10) *overlook / oversee* the project, matching the resources available to the (11) *requirements / requests* of 'the customer'.

Keep it on track The project manager is also responsible for making sure that the project is (12) *on / in* time and stays (13) *into / within* budget. This means (14) *confirming / checking* the progress of the work constantly.

3 Put each word in the correct form to complete the sentence.

0 He works for a *consultancy* firm.   CONSULT

1 We are known _____ for the quality of our products.   WORLD

2 What are the specific _____ of your customer?   REQUIRE

3 We don't need to advertise. We get a lot of _____ from other clients.   REFER

4 Customer _____ is very important to us.   SATISFY

5 We have a lot of _____ in this field.   EXPERT

6 She has a unique _____ of skills.   COMBINE

7 We are still waiting to know the _____ of their research.   COME

8 I have made an _____ for next Wednesday.   APPOINT

Pronunciation

4 Answer the following questions about word stress.

1 Look at where the stress falls in each of these words. What rule can you make?

organi**sa**tion   se**lec**tion   satis**fac**tion

com**mi**ssion

2 Mark the stress on these words.

combination   division   solution   installation

3 Study where the stress falls in each of these verbs.

de**vel**op   a**gree**   enter**tain**   re**quire**   ap**point**

in**vest**

4 Mark where the stress falls when each word is made into a noun by adding -*ment*.

development   agreement   entertainment

requirement   appointment   investment

5 What rule can you make?

Reporting

5 Change the highlighted verbs to reported speech.

Direct speech	Reported speech
I **am** too old	was
I **don't know**	
I **haven't seen** him	
You **have to** apply	
I **can** manage	
It**'s raining** here	
I **live** in Paris	
I **was waiting** for an hour	
I **won't** tell anyone	
I **can't** understand	

6 Read this brief report in a newspaper and answer the questions.

1 What will companies not be taxed on in the future?

2 What is the condition with works of art?

3 What will be the effect of the new law according to The Arts Council?

The government announced today that it would not tax spending on works of art bought by companies for public display. There would also be tax relief if companies sponsored other artistic events, such as theatre or dance productions. The Arts Council welcomed the announcement, saying that it would give a boost to the arts in Britain.

7 Read these statements given by spokespersons of various companies in response to this news. Rewrite them in reported speech.

0 'If it helps to promote the arts, we're for it.' (Tesco)
A spokesperson for Tesco said that if it helped to promote the arts, they were for it.

1 'It won't really affect us, as we do not sponsor any art projects anyway.' (Harris Plumbing)

2 'We are not against it, but I wish they would do the same for sports sponsorship.' (Riverside Centre)

3 'It's right for the government to reduce taxes on companies, but we have to decide where we can spend our money.' (Max's Café)

4 'It's about time. This government has a bad record on promoting the arts.' (Jones Gallery)

5 'I think this is a really good idea. It will help to bring art closer to the people.' (The Bus Company)

6 'I hope this will give employees a chance to show their artistic talents.' (Ashton Community Centre)

7 'It's not clear if this also applies to musical performances, but I hope so.' (Opera Now)

8 'Is it really true?' (Telecom)

8 Rewrite this reported announcement by a railway company in direct speech. Begin like this:

'We apologise for the inconvenience to passengers following ...'

The company apologised for the inconvenience to passengers, following the closure of the York to Newcastle line. This was due to an accident involving two freight trains. Fortunately, no-one had been injured. They said that the line would reopen on Tuesday morning after they had made repairs. In the meantime, passengers were asked to use other means of transport.

1 Complete the definitions by putting one word in each gap. The first letter has been given for you.

0 A formal speech at a meeting is called a
   presentation.

1 The person who runs the meeting is the
   c_____.

2 The person who takes the m_____ is the
   secretary.

3 The people who a_____ are the
   participants.

4 The list of items for discussion is the
   a_____.

5 An i_____ meeting is one between two or
   three people without these formal elements.

6 We call the reasons for h_____ the
   meeting the aims or objectives.

7 The objective is to r_____ an agreement
   on a decision by the end of the meeting.

8 When you state your opinion in a meeting, you
   make your p_____.

9 If others agree, they go a_____ with you.

10 Moving o_____ means stopping one
   subject and starting another.

2 Correct the underlined phrases in this extract from a meeting on reducing travel expenses.

Claudia OK. I think we have talked enough about
restaurants. Let's (0) go in *move on* to the next point,
which is the subject of flying.

Abdul Hang on. Have we (1) arrived in agreement
on which restaurants we can use?

Claudia Yes, I think we have agreed: no restaurants
unless it is for entertaining a client. Now, flying.
(2) It seems for me that people use business class
more than they need to.

Jordi (3) I am agree. It's not necessary for short
flights.

Claudia (4) I suggest us to make a rule that no-one
uses business class for a journey less than four hours.

Abdul (5) I disagree to you here. Sometimes we have
to arrive fresh for an early morning meeting.

Sara Can I just (6) go in here? In my experience, …

3 Read these comments by a manager on how he tries to make meetings more interesting and fun. Then answer the questions below.

1 Why does he use referee cards?

2 Why does he schedule the meeting 15 minutes
   early?

3 What does brain gymnastics help people to do?

4 Why does he ask participants to summarise the
   meeting in a picture?

5 Why does he sometimes cancel meetings?

When I chair a meeting, I always have two cards in my
top pocket – one yellow and one red – like a football
referee. If, during the meeting, someone says something
which is rude or too critical of another participant, I
show the yellow card, as a warning. It always makes
people smile and is a good way of avoiding any conflict
or tension.

I schedule the meeting about 15 minutes earlier than
we actually need to start. That way, it gives people an
opportunity to exchange a bit of small talk and relax
before proceedings become more formal. It's a simple
strategy but it works very well.

We sometimes do a little brain gymnastics at the
beginning of the meeting. That doesn't mean mental
mathematics or anything like that. It involves doing
physical exercises that help you to concentrate for
longer. The best known example is tapping your head
with one hand and at the same time making a circular
motion on your stomach with the other.

At the end of the meeting I ask each person to
summarise what they think they have learnt from it
and how it has benefited the company. But instead of
putting this in words, I ask them to draw a picture to
illustrate their point. The advantage of this is that it can
be funny and often people feel they can give their
opinion more openly.

One tactic I use, but not too often, is simply to cancel
the meeting and to ask the participants to spend the
time doing something other than their regular work.
For example, if the meeting was going to be about
marketing ideas, I might ask them to spend an hour
looking at other companies' websites or calling a friend
who works in another company to get ideas.

Report on a meeting

4 Look at this report on a meeting. It contains some mistakes. In most lines (not all) there is one extra word. If a line is correct, write CORRECT next to the line. If there is an extra word, write it in CAPITALS next to the line.

A report on the meeting to discuss travel expenses

0   The aim of the meeting was to look at with ways to reduce business travel expenses in the .... WITH

1   company. The discussion focussed on three main areas: restaurants, car hire and flying. ....

2   At the moment, there are no the rules about where and when it is acceptable to take a ....

3   business contact out for lunch in a restaurant. After some of discussion, we agreed that we ....

4   should use restaurants only when we do meet a client for the first time. For any other ....

5   occasions, the senior manager in the department must give his permission. The question of ....

6   car hire was more easier to solve. Claudia Hertz pointed out that the company could save ....

7   a lot of money simply by are negotiating a deal with one company for all our car hire. She ....

8   said that she would investigate this herself. The last point was the most difficult which to ....

9   reach agreement on. The participants disagreed about whether if it was necessary ....

10   to fly business class on short journeys. Most people agreed that they needed ....

11   to arrive fresh for meetings, but some the said the difference in comfort between economy ....

12   and business class did not have justify the extra expense. In the end, it was put to a vote ....

13   and the outcome was that in future all employees must to fly economy class for ....

14   journeys less than three hours long. If they want to fly business class on longer journeys ....
     they must get permission from the purchasing department.

5 Study the minutes of the meeting below and the additional notes written by a colleague. Write a full report including the information from the minutes and the additional notes. Organise your report as follows:

• title of report   • details of meeting   • what was discussed   • final action points

Minutes of meeting

Participants: Diego Sanchez, David Lyle,
                     Michiko Makio

Date: 14 July

Subject: Art commission

CEO would like to commission an artwork for the reception area of the new offices. Budget is £20,000.

DL said the cost of a consultant would have to come out of the budget, so it would be better to do it ourselves. Final decision: to employ a consultant for only half a day to help get ideas.

What type of artwork? All agreed that a sculpture would be best for the space.

Next step: MM agreed to make a list of possible artists to present at the next meeting.

DS asked if the work should reflect the image of the company. After discussion it was agreed that it was better to leave the character of the work to the artist himself.

Next meeting: 2 August

Some additional points –

• *Budget is <u>maximum</u> 20,000 but should be in region of 10,000*

• *DS to search for art consultant*

• *must write some suggestions for the artist for the next meeting*

1 Look at this list of tips for Part Two of the Speaking Test. Say which are true (T) and which are false (F).

1 You should speak in general terms and not give specific examples.

2 You should organise your talk: an introduction, main points and conclusion.

3 Separate each point clearly: *First, I think* ... , *Secondly, ... , Finally* ...

4 At the end, wait for the examiner to invite comments from your partner; don't ask them yourself.

5 Listen carefully to your partner's talk and be ready to agree or disagree with the points made.

6 When preparing your notes try to develop each argument as fully as possible.

2 Read this transcript of a candidate's mini-presentation. According to the answers in exercise 1, what are the good and bad points about it?

Shall I begin? OK, so the question is what are the important things thinking about when we choose a new supplier? For my view, there are three things we should consider:

The first is the price. The secondly is the quality of the supplies. And the third is the period of delivery. What I mean is the time it spends from ordering the supplies to the delivery into the factory or offices. In some industries, this must be a very important factor.

I think is very difficult to find a supplier who will can meet all of these conditions. For example, if the quality of the supplies is high, then probably the price will be also high.

I think that covers the main points. Do you have any questions, Paula?

3 These phrases from the presentation in exercise 2 contain grammatical or vocabulary mistakes. Try to correct them.

0 what are the important things thinking about
what are the important things to think about

1 For my view
_____

2 The secondly is the quality
_____

3 the third is the period of delivery
_____

4 the time it spends from
_____

5 the delivery into the factory
_____

6 In some industries, this must be a
_____

7 I think is very difficult
_____

8 who will can meet all of these conditions
_____

9 the price will be also high
_____

4 Complete the useful phrases for organising a mini-presentation by writing one word in each gap.

0 *So,* there are a number of points to consider ...
1 First of _____, ...
2 The second point to _____ is that ...
3 It is also true _____ many companies ...
4 Something _____ that is important is ...
5 _____ example, if you need to ...
6 _____ conclusion, I think ...

6.1 Recruitment

1 Complete this text by choosing the best word to fill each gap from A, B, C or D.

When giving (0) A on job interviews, we typically think of the job applicant and the types of things they need to know in order to get the job. However, the strength of the interviewer could make a big difference, and if you want to (1) _____ sure that you recruit the best person for the job, then the interviewer should also do their very best.

Preparation is (2) _____. You should be familiar with each applicant's CV and think carefully about the type of questions that will (3) _____ more about them. Asking the wrong question can waste time and give the applicant a false (4) _____ of you. Remember that the interviewer represents the company as a potential employer. It's the interviewer's role to convince the right candidate to take the job, and to be on the lookout for new (5) _____.

It's also your job to put a candidate at (6) _____ and create the right environment for them to perform to the best of their ability. Job interviews should not be about tripping people up or (7) _____ unnecessary stress. You can find out a lot more about a person by simply making the interview more like a conversation than an interrogation. Also encourage the person to ask you questions because these (8) _____ you a lot about the individual. Note also that it's unwise to rely solely on the interview. How the person writes a covering email with their CV, what their references are like and even (9) _____ they appear on social media will also affect your decision-making.

Finally, if you do decide to (10) _____ an application after the interview, then out of courtesy you should also let the candidate know. Also try to take time to give the candidate (11) _____ on the interview. It's good for your company's brand and it's always possible that this same candidate might learn from your comments and (12) _____ in a year's time and be the right person for the job.

0	A advice	B questions	
	C solutions	D suggestions	
1	A get	B do	
	C have	D make	
2	A priority	B first	
	C key	D main	
3	A discover	B inform	
	C reveal	D find	
4	A truth	B impression	
	C appearance	D represent	
5	A talent	B profession	
	C abilities	D performance	
6	A support	B comfortable	
	C safety	D ease	
7	A affecting	B resulting	
	C causing	D leading	
8	A say	B ask	
	C report	D tell	
9	A why	B how	
	C if	D when	
10	A advertise	B reject	
	C recruit	D interview	
11	A feedback	B rejection	
	C appraisal	D information	
12	A refer	B recruit	
	C reapply	D reverse	

2 Choose the best ending A–I to complete the sentences about employment.

0	We try to recruit	A	twenty people in the last two years.
1	He was fired for	B	on without a formal interview.
2	I was so angry that I just walked	C	because the company offered an excellent package.
3	I took voluntary redundancy	D	you must give at least one month's notice.
4	We have hired	E	out there and then.
5	He resigned	F	only the best graduates.
6	Three hundred people were laid off	G	sleeping on the job.
7	If you want to leave	H	because he didn't agree with the company's sales strategy.
8	They took me	I	when the plant closed.

3 Choose the right word or phrase to answer these questions.

1 Jack was late for work every day last week. Is he going to be **made redundant** or be **dismissed**?

2 Joe is 65. Is he going to **retire** or **resign** from the company?

3 Is the company running a campaign to **recruit** or to **hire** young people?

4 Sarah has had a job offer from another company. Is she going to **leave** her present company or **take voluntary redundancy**?

Pronunciation

4 The underlined words have the same sound. Match each pair with the word in the box that sounds most similar.

| tyre fine fork stayed ~~boot~~ look |

0 It <u>suits</u> the new <u>recruits</u>. *boot*

1 I didn't <u>resign</u> from the <u>design</u> department.

2 They <u>laid</u> off the <u>maid</u>.

3 I <u>took</u> your <u>book</u>.

4 We <u>walked</u> and <u>talked</u>.

5 They have a <u>hire</u> and <u>fire</u> policy.

Passives

5 Look at these notices at a company's site and say where you would find them.

1 THIS PARKING SPACE IS RESERVED FOR CUSTOMERS

2 Protective glasses must be worn at all times in this area

3 *Visitors are asked to sign the visitors' book*

4 Stop button: to be pressed in emergencies only

5 NB. Staff party has been moved to 2 December

6 Transform these statements into notices in the passive.

0 Keep this door locked at all times.
This door to be kept locked at all times.

1 The union invites all members to attend a meeting on Friday 12 July.

2 You should report anything suspicious to security immediately.

3 You can post suggestions in this box.

4 Queen Elizabeth opened this building in 1988.

5 You must obtain a registration form from the Administration Office.

7 Put these newspaper headlines into full sentences. Use passive or active verb forms.

0 **300 LAID OFF AT LONGBRIDGE PLANT**
300 employees have been laid off at the Longbridge plant.

1 **HOLBROKE SACKED BY CAPITAL INVESTORS**

2 **400 JOBS TO BE CREATED IN NORTH WEST**

3 **CEO RESIGNS AFTER RECORD LOSSES ANNOUNCED AT TELEAST**

4 **Temporary workers given only 1 day's notice**

5 **REPORT SHOWS 300 NEW DOCTORS NEEDED**

6 ENGLAND FOOTBALL MANAGER RESIGNS

8 Transform these active sentences into the passive.

0 I expect the company to tell me in good time if there are going to be redundancies.
I expect to be told in good time ...

1 It's better for people to respect you than to like you.

2 I dislike people telling me what to do.

3 It's nice when the company considers you for a promotion.

4 I don't like it when people keep me waiting.

5 I don't mind people questioning my decisions.

6.2 Electronic communication

1 **Read this article about a time management technique. Choose the best sentence A–G to fill each gap 1–5. One example is given and one sentence is not needed.**

Since the invention of electronic communication, including email, phone texts and online chat messaging, workers have been complaining that they seem to have less and less time to get things done. (0) F Most of us are probably not unused to that feeling of being interrupted in the middle of our work by a computer notification that an urgent email has arrived. Or perhaps our phones are vibrating loudly on our desks from time to time to inform us that a text message has landed in our inbox. On top of that, those who forget to change their status on social platforms such as Skype™ or Facetime, are probably aware that anyone could call them up for a face-to-face conversation at any time. (1) _____

As a result of this modern assault on our working lives, time management has become the number one issue for many workers. Many complain of feeling that their working day is increasingly under pressure from an endless stream of interruptions. (2) _____ It was invented by Francesco Cirillo and works like this: You break your working day up into 25-minute periods. You work for 25 minutes, then take a break for five minutes. Every period of 25 minutes is called a 'Pomodoro' after the Italian word for tomato. (Cirillo originally used a kitchen timer that was shaped like a tomato.) (3) _____

Believers in this technique say that it makes you concentrate more effectively while working. (4) _____ Some people even create a to-do list to go with this technique, and after each 25-minute period, they put a tick next to a completed item. Not everyone finds the technique easy at first and it's been pointed out that you will need to practise the Pomodoro technique for a few days before it becomes instinctive to you. (5) _____ However, even if you don't decide to follow the Pomodoro technique exactly as it's defined, perhaps its basic concept of setting aside specific periods for full concentration on a specific task is something worth trying.

A Many people have reported success with this technique but others cannot see the benefits.

B One way to help people manage their time better is the Pomodoro technique.

C As a result of this constant barrage of interruptions, it's unsurprising if people forget what they were working on in the first place.

D Also, you will need to remember to switch off your computer or phone notifications, in order to avoid being distracted by any pop-ups, chimes or other alerts.

E After you have completed four 'Pomodoros', ie four periods of 25 minutes, you can take a longer 15-minute break.

F It seems that modern technology, instead of making our lives easier, has increased the pace of life for many of us and has made it harder for people to concentrate.

G For people who work on many different projects at the same time, it's also a way to compartmentalise each different project into fixed periods of time.

2 **Read these short email messages and complete the text by writing an appropriate verb in each gap.**

●●●

Dear Alice

I am sorry that I haven't been in touch. My computer crashed yesterday and I wasn't able to (0) *read* my emails.

●●●

Davina

I'm sorry, but I (1) _____ your last email by mistake. Can you (2) _____ it, please?

●●●

John

Sorry, I (3) _____ to attach the file to my last email. Here it is. Please let me (4) _____ that you have received it.

●●●

Dear Ivan

Thank you for sending me the link to the Sparks website. It doesn't seem to (5) _____, though. Can you (6) _____ that it's the correct address?

●●●

Dear Mr Cousins

I sent you an email about your account with us last Friday, but I haven't (7) _____ a reply.

●●●

Dear Yi

Here is your username and password so that you can (8) _____ the site. Just (9) _____ them in when you are asked and then (10) _____ on the link to Case Histories.
Good luck

Paul

Internal communication

3 Choose the best ending A–J to complete the sentences.

0	Please note that	A	your recent memo about absenteeism.
1	I would appreciate	B	these new regulations will not come into effect until May.
2	I am writing with regard to	C	if you could make sure that everyone is aware of the changes.
3	I'd like to remind	D	everyone that the plant will be closed for maintenance.
4	I'm sorry	E	your help with this.
5	The reasons	F	for your comments.
6	I'd be grateful	G	a meeting of the board on Tuesday, it has been decided to …
7	Following	H	for the changes are as follows:
8	Please	I	for the inconvenience this will cause.
9	Thank you	J	submit your suggestions by Friday.

4 A colleague has sent you her presentation to look through before she gives it at a conference next week. It contains several mistakes. Write a short email to her to explain this and to suggest a meeting so that you can go through it together. Use the framework given.

• • •

Dear Liane

Thank you for _____

I have looked _____

Unfortunately, it _____

Perhaps we _____

Let me know _____

5 Complete the internal memos by putting one word in each gap.

┌─────────────────────────────────────┐
│ ▭▭▭▭▭▭▭▭▭▭▭▭▭ **INTERNAL MEMO** │

To: All office staff

From: Wanda Koepchen

RE: Coffee area

(0) Following comments from various members of staff about the untidiness of the coffee area, I'd like to (1) _____ all staff that visitors are also taken to this area from time to time. If it is not kept clean, it gives a bad impression of the company to outsiders. In future (2) _____ make sure that you clean your coffee cups and leave the area looking tidy.

I (3) _____ your help with this.

INTERNAL MEMO

Dear Wanda

I am writing with (4) _____ to your memo about the coffee area. I understand your concerns, but I think the (5) _____ for the untidiness is not the staff being careless. The fact is that the room hasn't been painted for four years and there is no proper coffee machine in it. I'd be (6) _____ if you could ask the management to consider investing in making these improvements to the coffee area.

Geraldine

INTERNAL MEMO

Dear Geraldine

Thank you for your (7) _____.
I have made a (8) _____ of them
and will pass them on to the management.

6.3 Reading Test: Part Two

1 Each pair of sentences below is missing a connecting sentence. Write a sentence that fits grammatically and in meaning, using the idea in brackets.

0 Don't wait for all the conditions to be right. They never will be. (never) Try to be satisfied that just the important ones have been met.

1 There are various ways to recruit someone for a high-level job. (advertise / newspaper)

_____

Another is to use a head-hunting firm.

2 First, ask yourself these basic questions. (enjoy / job?)

_____

And are there better opportunities elsewhere?

3 Wayne Sanders also expressed his concerns about the plan. (I think / design / weaknesses)

'_____

Besides', he added, 'no-one will invest in it.'

4 The first version was well received although it had some minor design faults. (second / improvement)

_____

And the third is expected to be even better.

5 The results were not at all what the researchers expected. (77 per cent / very unhappy)

_____

While only 23 per cent said they were satisfied with the level of service.

6 Having the security of a job for life used to be considered fairly normal 30 years ago. (nowadays / same job / ten years)

_____

But there are signs that this kind of long-term relationship between employer and employee may be coming back into fashion.

2 Read the article about volunteering and choose the best sentences from A–G to fill each gap 1–5. One example is given and one sentence is not needed.

A Such volunteers work in welfare organisations in aid of causes that they believe in.

B Such work often allows people to gain experience in a dream job or in a company of their choice.

C Volunteer work is a good way to build up skills and experience for those who lack work experience.

D The retiree, for instance, is someone you'd often spot doing volunteer work.

E Not all volunteer work will be useful to you so select carefully.

F And perhaps, just as importantly, you will also start to build a network of contacts related to the area you are interested in.

G Some people volunteer on a weekend or on their days off.

These days more of us are volunteering than ever before. (0) *G* Others may volunteer more frequently, as they have plenty of free time and a strong desire to help. (1) _____ Such a person may no longer need to work but it doesn't mean that they're willing to take it easy, as they feel that they have plenty of experience and energy still to give. (2) _____

However, volunteering isn't just for older people who don't want to spend all day at home in front of the TV. More young people these days are doing voluntary work either overseas or in their own local community. (3) _____ It looks great on a CV and it is also a good way to get valuable references from the other people you work with.

Volunteer work can be done at the workplace, too. (4) _____ Though the work may be done for free, in return, you'd get to work alongside and learn from experienced colleagues, and gain clearer insight into the company's culture. (5) _____. Whichever type of volunteering you choose, remember that your volunteer work doesn't always have to match the job that you wish to do in future, but that it should allow you to hone the skills that could benefit you in future.

7.1 Job qualities

1 Read the statements made by different salespeople and choose the best phrase for each gap.

| tangible results   ~~cold calling~~ |
| door-to-door selling   sales pitch   target-driven |
| sales techniques |

0 *Cold calling* is very difficult. Half the time people just put the phone down when they realise you are trying to sell something.

1 It's very important to practise your _____ until it is perfect. You only get one opportunity to convince people.

2 Actually, I think that _____ is an invasion of someone's privacy. I don't think it should be allowed.

3 Our company is very _____. We all have monthly objectives and our pay is closely linked to these.

4 The great thing about sales work is that you have _____. In a lot of jobs, it's difficult to measure your contribution.

5 There are a lot of different _____ but the basic principle is always the same: you have to convince people that they need and want what you are selling.

2 Decide whether these adjectives describing the job of selling are positive or negative, and write them in the correct column in the table.

| dishonest   rewarding   unglamorous |
| dynamic   well-paid   challenging   tangible |
| unpopular   sociable   repetitive |

Positive	Negative
	dishonest

3 Put each word in the correct form to complete the sentences about selling.

0 Selling can be a very *challenging* job.
CHALLENGE

1 But it can also be very _____.
REWARD

2 And it can be _____ when people don't buy.   FRUSTRATE

3 People say that it must be a _____ job.   REPEAT

4 But in fact, it has a lot of _____.
VARY

5 You meet many _____ people.
INTEREST

6 I never suffer from _____.   BORE

7 Also I have _____ for my own decisions.   RESPONSIBLE

8 And I am _____ for what I do.
GOOD PAY

Pronunciation

4 In the word 'dishonest' the letter 'h' is <u>not</u> pronounced. Underline the letter in these words which is not pronounced.

debt	autumn	environment
whole	business	mortgage
knowledge	guard	hour
wrong	listen	building
doubt	climb	

Comparatives and superlatives

5 Complete the table of comparative and superlative forms.

Adjective (or adverb)	Comparative form	Superlative form
high	higher	the highest
low		
good	better	
well		
bad		the worst
flexible	more flexible	
rich		the richest
far	further	
pretty		
boring		
little		the least
much	more	

6 Complete the sentences describing the advantages of different jobs by writing one word in each gap.

0 I do a little extra consulting outside my regular job. I don't earn much from it but it's *better* than nothing.

1 _____ best aspect of the job is the feeling that I am making a real difference.

2 Job satisfaction is more important to me _____ money.

3 The hours are _____ flexible than in most jobs and that suits me.

4 If you have a positive attitude, then selling is as easy _____ any other job.

5 New York is an expensive place to live, but London is _____ more expensive.

6 If you include commissions and bonuses, then a sales job is _____ paid than a job in marketing.

7 It's the _____ challenging job I've ever had, but I am loving every minute of it.

8 It's been a very difficult time for the company, but I suppose things can't get any _____.

7 Look at this text about price comparison websites. It contains ten mistakes (one in each line) with comparative and superlative forms. Correct the mistakes.

0 A last time you bought a washing machine, how did you go about it? I wouldn't be   *The last time*

1 surprised if you did the same thing than me. First, I searched on the Internet to find out   _____

2 more about the subject: which one was the reliablest, which one was the most efficient,   _____

3 and so on. Having done this, I then looked for the better price I could find for the model   _____

4 I had chosen. And then? Did I order it online? No. I went to my nearer electrical shop so   _____

5 that I could have a more close look at the machine before I bought it. I just used the   _____

6 traditional shop to inspect the product before buying, like so more people these days. I had   _____

7 no intention of buying a machine there, because I thought the price would be highest than   _____

8 online. In fact, surprisingly it turned out to be just as cheaper in the shop. So I bought it. It   _____

9 seems that retailers have been forced to offer similar prices with the Internet competition to   _____

10 avoid going out of business. I don't know how they do this, because their overhead costs are many higher, but I'm glad, because I still prefer to shop in the traditional way.   _____

7.2 Selling

1 Complete this crossword about the elements necessary to make a successful sale.

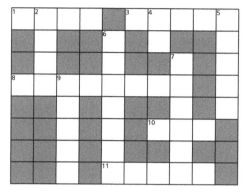

1 across You must be prepared to _____ sometimes. All sales people suffer knockbacks. (4)

3 across and 5 down A good salesperson _____ his _____. In other words, he understands the product he is selling. (5, 5)

8 across Don't just describe the product, explain to the customer what its _____ are to him. (8)

10 across The customer will _____ from you if they feel the product will make their life better. (3)

2 down It's not true that a good salesperson is _____ to sell anything to anyone. (4)

4 down If a customer says _____ at first, don't give up. (2)

5 down see 3 across

6 down Don't impose your own personality on the customer. Try to _____ his personality. (7)

7 down Ask questions to find out what _____ are important to the customer. (6)

8 down and 11 across Before you can sell anything you have to _____ the _____ of the customer. If they think you are dishonest, they will not buy from you. (5,5)

9 down You have to persuade the customer that he really _____ the product. (5)

2 Look at each conversation between a customer and a salesperson and choose the best word to fill each gap.

0 **Customer** Sorry, I don't understand why you don't have the item I want (in)/ *on* stock.
Salesperson We don't carry a big range at this time of year because *supply / (demand)* falls a lot.

1 **Customer** I'm interested *by / in* a new camera.
Salesperson OK. What kind of camera did you have in *your mind / mind*? Compact or professional?

2 **Customer** What colours does it *go / come* in?
Salesperson We have this model in red and black. The *outdated / updated* version is silver.

3 **Customer** The last lamps we bought from you didn't *prove / approve* to be very popular with our customers.
Salesperson I think perhaps the design was a little complicated. This new range is a huge improvement *to / on* last year's.

4 **Customer** I'm really not sure about these. I'll think *about / of* it and let you know.
Salesperson Why don't I just *take / put* you down for a small order then?

5 **Customer** I like these. How *many / much* would it cost to have our logo on them?
Salesperson I can't *make / give* you a price on that just now, but I'll check with the office and call you this afternoon.

6 **Salesperson** Hello, Mrs Gardener. I don't want to take up much of your time, but I was *considering / wondering* if I could interest you in a fantastic broadband offer.
Customer Thank you, but we're happy *with / in* the service that we have already.

3 What verbs are possible in each of these expressions?

1 To _____ customer needs

2 To _____ a sale

3 To _____ two similar products

4 To _____ a proposal

5 To _____ the benefits

A proposal

4 Read the proposal below and choose the best sentence A–H to fill each gap.

Dear Mr Tang

(0) F I understand that you have already looked at our website. (1) _____ I suggest as a first step that I visit you at your headquarters at a convenient date. (2) _____ We can also discuss your exact requirements. (3) _____ This quotation will be free of charge. (4) _____

At the moment we are offering a 20 per cent discount on two of the ranges. (5) _____ If you wish to consider this option, please contact me without delay. (6) _____ Thank you once again for contacting Aquadream.

(7) _____

Kind regards

Tomas Herzberg

A It also puts you under no obligation to order from us.

B As you will have seen, as well as supplying showers, we provide a full installation service.

C I have put my personal number at the top of the page.

D When I know these, I can prepare a formal proposal and estimate.

E I will bring with me brochures of the various ranges we offer.

F Thank you for your enquiry about showers for your hotel.

G I look forward to hearing from you in the very near future.

H However, please note that this offer will end on 30 June.

5 You work for an office relocation services company. You receive the following enquiry. Read it and answer the questions.

1 What is good about their present offices?

2 In what way do they not meet the company's requirements?

3 What do they need more of?

4 What information would Mr Smith like to receive in reply?

Dear Sir

We are a small, but growing company that provides a range of computer services: website design, database management and software training. There are sixteen of us in total. At the moment we work from rented offices in the centre of the city. This has been quite convenient up to now, as many of our clients are also in the city. However, the offices are becoming too small for us and the building is not well equipped for our line of work. In addition, more and more of our business is coming from companies outside the city.

Consequently, we would like to find larger premises (at least 1,000 m²) in a more modern building and in a location that is easy to reach and has good parking facilities.

Can you let me know if you can help us in this and also what your fees are?

Kind regards

Jasper Smith

---

6 Write the reply to Mr Smith's enquiry in exercise 5 using the framework below.

Dear Mr Smith

Thank you for _____

We would be delighted _____

At the moment we have two suitable _____

One is _____ Its key features are: _____

The other is an attractive _____ Its advantages are that: _____

Full details of our fees can be _____

Please do not hesitate _____

I look forward _____

7.3 Reading Test: Part Four

Exam Tip

This part of the exam tests your knowledge of vocabulary. Usually that means choosing the word with the correct meaning. But it is also necessary that the word fits grammatically in the sentence.

1 Choose the word that does NOT fit grammatically in these sentences.

0 Only two companies were _____ to participate in the trial.

A prepared   (B interested)

C willing   D happy

1 Consequently they _____ to share the costs.

A decided   B agreed

C considered   D promised

2 It is a _____ of the contract that customers pay within 30 days.

A condition   B requirement

C term   D ask

3 This is not the _____ time that this happened.

A secondly   B first

C last   D longest

4 On average someone goes out of business every _____ minutes.

A three   B few

C many   D ten

5 _____ of selling is very useful in this kind of job.

A Awareness   B Experience

C Opportunity   D Knowledge

2 Read the text below about advertising. Choose the best word to fill each gap from A, B, C or D.

The first task is not to select the right advertising (0) B, but to choose the right message. Advertisements (1) _____ assume that the reader, listener or viewer has a basic level of interest and is (2) _____ close attention to the ad. But customers (3) _____ to ignore all ads that do not speak directly to them. For this to be the (4) _____, the product or service you are promoting has to meet a (5) _____ of the consumer. (6) _____ you have established this, then you can concentrate on how to deliver the message. Remember: the message has to be clear and simple.

In (7) _____ to answer the question of where you should place your advertisement, you will need to consider the following. First, how long is the (8) _____ going to last? If you want to raise the general awareness of your brand, you will need time and money. These are resources which not (9) _____ small or medium-sized businesses have. The (10) _____ is short-term advertisements: for example, offering a product at a (11) _____ price for a limited period. The problem with this is that, even if the message (12) _____ to people at the time, customers will quickly erase the advertisement from their memories.

	A	B	C	D
0	place	(medium)	promoting	newspaper
1	usually	general	most	do
2	making	give	paying	in
3	think	are	often	tend
4	means	case	true	fact
5	request	need	client	will
6	Before	Soon	As	Once
7	how	case	time	order
8	way	best	campaign	time
9	many	long	time	far
10	way	alternative	other	better
11	cheaply	reduced	down	money
12	gets on	takes over	sets up	gets through

8.1   Training

1 Read the article on training and choose the best word to fill each gap from A, B, C or D.

A lot of managers question the usefulness of employees (0) B courses which are not directly related to their sector or job function. For example, the skills (1) _____ to be a salesman are knowledge of the product, the ability to persuade and the ability to listen and read (2) _____ from the buyer. What would you do if a salesman asked if he could (3) _____ on a course entitled 'How to Improve your Concentration through Yoga'? Would you say 'No' (4) _____ ? Would you say, 'OK, but not on company time or at the company's (5) _____ '? Or would you stop to (6) _____ about how this might benefit the company and individual in a wider sense? Apart from the obvious (7) _____ opportunities, there are other advantages to employees following courses which don't focus only (8) _____ work-related subjects. The employee will feel greater loyalty to the company if he is encouraged to (9) _____ other interests and improve himself through training. Often the experience itself, or something the (10) _____ said, will have given him a new idea or fresh perspective on his work. Invariably, he will return to work with renewed motivation.

0	A making	B doing	
	C getting	D going	
1	A necessarily	B responsible	
	C required	D trained	
2	A books	B come	
	C signals	D about	
3	A pay	B application	
	C be	D enrol	
4	A directly	B idea	
	C to	D ever	
5	A place	B expense	
	C pay	D money	
6	A consider	B imagine	
	C discuss	D think	
7	A networking	B possibilities	
	C and	D take	
8	A in	B at	
	C on	D about	
9	A involve	B explore	
	C showing	D go	
10	A book	B priest	
	C professor	D tutor	

2 Decide whether each phrase in the box describes an advantage or a disadvantage and write it in the correct column in the table.

| a plus   the downside   one drawback |
| one good thing   one problem   a benefit |
| one thing against   a positive point |

Advantage	Disadvantage
a plus	

Pronunciation

Pronunciation Tip

↘ Falling: Intonation falls at the end of statements and *Wh-* questions.

↗ Rising: Intonation rises in *yes / no* questions and when we leave a sentence unfinished.

↘↗ Fall-rise: Intonation falls at first but rises at the end if we want to show doubt or uncertainty.

3 Mark each sentence in this dialogue with the correct arrows to show the intonation.

0 **A** I'm very worried that a lot of middle managers don't understand finance. ↘

00 **B** Should we organise some training for them? ↗

1 **A** Yes, maybe a little basic training would help.

2 **B** What kind of training did you have in mind?

3 **A** Well, although face-to-face training is expensive ...

4 **B** You think it is more effective.

5 **A** Yes, don't you?

6 **B** Actually there are some very good computer-based financial training programmes.

7 **A** One advantage is that it would be more flexible.

8 **B** Yes, and another good thing about it is that they might agree to do it from home, I suppose.

9 **A** OK. Can you get me some more information about these courses?

10 **B** Sure. When will you need it by?

-ing form and infinitive

4 Decide whether each verb phrase is followed by the -ing form or the infinitive, or whether both are possible. Complete the table.

> remember   afford   stop   involve   like
> want   would like   recommend   start
> prefer   be interested in

+-*ing* form	+ infinitive (to do)	Both possible
		remember

5 Here are some internal messages from a company's intranet. Circle the correct verb form to complete each one.

● ● ●

1
John would like *speaking* / (*to speak*) to you about a recent order. Please remember *calling* / *to call* him.

2
Sorry Nadia, I don't remember *seeing* / *to see* your laptop when we got off the train. I suggest *calling* / *to call* the station.

3
Sorry you are having problems with the new software. You can probably retrieve the information by *switching* / *to switch* the computer off and *restarting* / *to restart* it.

4
I've stopped *using* / *to use* Heal and Co. The quality of their service has really gone down since the new management took over.

5
Please can you make your letter a little more polite? I know it's their mistake, but we can't afford *risking* / *to risk* upsetting them.

6
Are you interested in *attending* / *to attend* this conference? If so, please let me know. I am attaching the details.

7
Would you like *coming* / *to come* with me to a concert on Saturday? I've got a spare ticket.

6 Complete the sentences about yourself using a gerund or an infinitive.

1 I'm very interested _____
_____.

2 In my free time, I like _____
_____.

3 At the moment, I can't afford _____
_____.

4 If you come to my country, I recommend _____
_____.

5 Generally, for breakfast I like _____
_____.

6 When I was 16, I remember _____
_____.

7 My work mainly involves _____
_____.

8 When travelling, I prefer _____
_____.

9 When I retire, I would like _____
_____.

7 Write the missing words to complete the spider chart showing ways of delivering training.

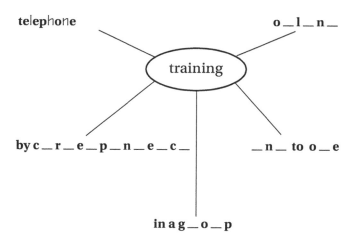

telephone

o _ l _ n _

training

by c _ r _ e _ p _ n _ e _ c _

_ n _ to o _ e

in a g _ o _ p

8.2 Showing you're listening

1 Read the five characteristics of bad listeners and answer the questions below.

● ● ●

Bad listeners:

- Give advice. In fact most people just want you to listen. If they want advice they will generally ask for it.
- Are defensive. They see most discussions as a debate which they should try to win. This closes their minds to other viewpoints.
- Interrupt. They make judgements too quickly on what they think others are saying and then come in with their own opinion.
- Want to go one step better. Instead of responding to what they hear, they respond with a story of their own which is 'better' than the other person's.
- Don't empathise. They think that the speaker's feelings are wrong, when in fact each person's feelings are equally valid, even if they are different from yours.

1 Why is it a bad idea to give advice?

A People usually don't want it.

B People tend not to follow others' advice.

C It's difficult to understand another person's situation.

2 Why do people interrupt?

A Because they think the other person has bad judgement.

B Because they think they have understood before the speaker has finished.

C Because they think it is a normal part of conversation.

3 What is said about people's feelings?

A Everyone's feelings are different.

B Everyone's feelings should be respected.

C They will probably be different from yours.

2 Mark the following sentences with + if they show sensitivity in the speaker, or – if they show you are more interested in speaking than listening.

0 Let me just stop you there. ☐−

1 Yes, I see what you mean. ☐

2 So, if I understand you correctly, you're saying that … ☐

3 And how did you feel about that? ☐

4 I'll tell you what I think. ☐

5 That reminds me of the time when I … ☐

6 Are you really? That's interesting. ☐

7 Why do you think that is? ☐

8 Well, of course, I think the answer is obvious. ☐

9 That's funny, because in my job I have to … ☐

3 What do the + phrases in exercise 2 have in common? And the – phrases?

4 Look at the prompt card from Part 3 of the Speaking Test and the transcript of two candidates discussing the topic from the card. They make some mistakes (which are underlined). Correct them.

Induction Day

Your company would like to arrange a welcome and induction day for a group of new recruits. You have been asked to contribute some ideas. Discuss with your partner:

- what this day could include
- how you can make the new recruits feel at home.

Student A So we need looking *to look* at what kind of induction training we can give to new recruits. I think that a general tour and a presentation of the company's history would be a good idea. What (1) are you think?

Student B Yes, I'd go along (2) to that. And I'd recommend (3) to put them in small groups for the tour so that there is an opportunity for them to ask as many questions (4) than they want.

Student A I think you're right, but we may not have enough (5) of experienced staff for this.

Student B Well, another option (6) can be to have a kind of buddy system.

Student A Sorry … I'm not sure (7) to know what you mean. Could you explain?

Student B Yes. It's when you put each new (8) recruits with an experienced employee so that they can follow them and ask (9) questions to them when necessary.

Student A (10) That's sounds like a good idea. I think the advantage would be that the new recruits will feel (11) most comfortable in a one-to-one situation. And what about welcoming them? What do you suggest (12) to do?

Linking phrases

5 Match each of the conjunctions 1–5 with a more formal linking phrase A–F which has a similar meaning.

0 After	A Due to
1 So	B In addition to this
2 Even so	C However
3 But	D Following
4 Also	E As a result of this
5 Because of	F In spite of this

6 Rewrite each sentence using the phrase given so that it has the same meaning as the first sentence.

0 We don't have a very big budget for training, but we do more than in many companies.
Despite *not having a big budget for training, we do more than in many companies.*

1 It's a very effective training course. Furthermore, it can be done in only two days.
In addition to _____
_____

2 The session had to be cancelled because the weather was bad.
Because of _____
_____

3 Only six people enrolled on the course. Nevertheless, it went ahead anyway.
Despite _____
_____

4 After we had discussed the issue, we took a vote.
Following _____
_____

7 Choose the linking phrases from the list below to complete this letter.

> nevertheless   however   ~~following~~   despite
> moreover   in addition to   due to   as a result
> unfortunately

Dear Ms O'Dwyer

(0) Following a meeting of the Finance committee last month, it has been decided to cut our training budget by 20 per cent next year.

(1) _____, the HR department has had to make some difficult decisions about which programmes will be affected.

(2) _____, your two-day course on cross-cultural issues is one of those we have decided to cancel, (3) _____ its popularity with the staff. (4) _____, the good news is that we would still like to continue with your 'Effective Communications' course.

(5) _____, it is possible that we would like to run three, rather than two of these courses next year.

Please can you send me a full proposal (including prices) for these courses.

(6) _____ this, we will need three references. I am sorry for all the extra work – this is also (7) _____ a decision of the board to improve the process of commissioning training. (8) _____, I am confident that you will be given the contract.

I appreciate your understanding and look forward to hearing from you.

Yours sincerely

Jackson Nesmith

1 Look at these transcripts from the Listening Test and answer questions 1–5. Underline the key words in the text that gave you the answer.

**Section One
(Questions 1–5)**

- You will hear five short recordings where people talk about their work.
- For each recording, decide what job the speaker does.
- Choose from the list below (A–H).

1 _____
2 _____
3 _____
4 _____
5 _____

A Salesperson
B Production manager
C Personal assistant
D Receptionist
E Marketing manager
F Company doctor
G Recruitment officer
H Trainer

1

Of course knowledge of your subject is important, but when you're teaching people the key is to understand that not everyone learns in the same way, or at the same speed. So you have to accept this and not get frustrated if someone seems to be taking longer to understand a point.

2

There are a lot of books about management theory, but for me it's all down to one thing: the ability to distinguish between what's urgent and important and what isn't. We have a lot of different advertising projects and promotions going on at any one time and I have to decide what needs working on now and what can wait.

3

No one likes rejection, but in my line of work you have to accept that sometimes people are going to say 'no'. The critical point is how you deal with failure. If you don't remain optimistic and move on to the next customer or prospect with enthusiasm, then you're not going to get very far.

4

I've been very lucky in that my bosses have always been nice, patient types. I've been working for the same boss now for nine years, keeping her diary, organising her travel and making sure she always has the right information to hand. I see my main role as trying to keep everything in order for her so that she can approach her work feeling calm and supported.

5

There are not so many of us any more. I think only a few big companies still have an internal medical service. That's a shame because the health of the staff has a big effect on morale. Also, if you have a lot of people absent through sickness it can really affect the bottom line. My role is to be aware of what the current health issues and risks are and to take action to prevent these hurting the company. So I spend most of my time listening to people and gathering information.

2 Now answer exam questions 6–10 below using the transcripts 1–5 from exercise 1. (Remember that in the exam you will have **different** recordings for the second part.) Underline the words or phrases in the text that gave you the answer.

**Section Two
(Questions 6–10)**

- You will hear five short recordings where people talk about their work.
- For each recording, decide which skill they identify as the most important for this job from the list below (A–H).

6 _____
7 _____
8 _____
9 _____
10 _____

A To be organised
B To be creative
C To be able to prioritise
D To be friendly
E To network
F To be a good listener
G To be patient
H To have a positive attitude

9.1 Branding

Brands

1 Complete the marketing collocations using the words in the box.

> identity   marketing   packaging   ~~billboard~~
> impact   advertising   customer

0   billboard advertising

1   brand _____

2   _____ slogan

3   big _____

4   _____ perception

5   attractive _____

6   _____ tool

2 Complete the slogans for these brands using the words in the box.

> local   quality   ultimate

1   _____ never goes out of style.

2   The world's _____ bank

3   The _____ driving machine

3 Which slogan from exercise 2 is about:

1   lifestyle?

2   quality?

3   scale of operation?

4 Look at the statements below and the article about American brands. Which of the paragraphs (A–D) does each statement (0–6) refer to? You will need to use some of the letters more than once.

0   To sell products in other countries you need to be aware of their cultures. A

1   People do not want products which promote an American way of life any more. _____

2   The American brands which have been successful are the ones which have adapted their products to the local market. _____

3   Americans do not make enough visits to the international markets they sell into. _____

4   Some US companies have understood the need to win the confidence of local customers. _____

5   Political decisions have damaged US brands. _____

6   American education programmes are becoming more international. _____

A

The USA controls one third of the global economy. Its brands have enormous influence in markets all over the world. But with this comes a responsibility to be sensitive to other cultures. This means travelling to other countries and acquiring cultural knowledge. However, Americans have a poor record of going abroad to research foreign markets and only 40 per cent of the population hold passports.

B

But they have begun to realise that they need to adapt the identities of their brands to the local market. The war in Iraq and other policies made the USA less popular internationally and this certainly hurt some of the well-known brands, like Coca-Cola™ and McDonald's™, which represent American culture.

C

But there are some US companies which, for some time, have enjoyed greater success: Heinz, Ford, Kellogg's, General Motors. What do they have in common? They try to understand their local markets and build trust with local consumers. They get their raw materials from local suppliers and they recruit their managers from the countries they operate in. They support local charities and community projects. Moreover, they change their products so that they suit local tastes.

D

The world still wants American products, but not necessarily an American lifestyle. In schools more international geography is being taught, and in business schools more international marketing case studies are being used. Most importantly, American companies are listening more to their international consumers and business partners.

Relative clauses

5 Complete the relative clauses in this letter by writing either *who, which, whose, where, when* or *why* in each space.

Dear Ms Haratounian

Thank you for your letter (0) which was passed to me today, concerning the air conditioning system (1) _____ we installed for you in March. I am sorry for the delay in replying, but the person (2) _____ job it is to deal with after sales enquiries is away at the moment.

I understand that on hot days, (3) _____ you would like to lower the temperature, it does not go down far enough. From your description, I think the reason (4) _____ the system is not working properly is that the engineer (5) _____ programmed it set the master controls too high. This is how to fix the problem:

Go to the main control box and next to the place (6) _____ it says 'MASTER TEMP' you will find two buttons: a blue one (7) _____ makes the air colder, and a red one to make it hotter. Press the blue button until the counter reaches 10. This should fix the problem.

If you have any difficulties or if there is something you don't understand, please feel free to call me at the office or on my mobile (8) _____ is always switched on.

Kind regards

Abdul Aziz

6 For each sentence decide if *which* or *who* is necessary or if it can be omitted.

0 It's the strategy which I feel most comfortable with.
   Omitted: It's the strategy I feel most comfortable with.

1 I can't decide which is the best one to buy.

2 It is the first new product which we have launched in six years.

3 The Nestlé™ strategy is to buy brands which are already established.

4 We design our own advertisements, which is a cheaper solution.

5 Alborn, which is the world's leading brand consultancy, has agreed to work with us.

6 The company which we used last year has gone out of business.

7 I can't decide which is the best way to get there.

8 He's a man who I respect very much.

7 Complete the sentences with a defining relative clause.

0 She's the kind of person who would do anything for anyone.

1 New York is the kind of place _____
   _____

2 Your 20's are a period in your life _____
   _____

3 My parents are the reason _____
   _____

4 It's the kind of book _____
   _____

5 The iPhone™ is the kind of product _____
   _____

6 He's the kind of manager _____
   _____

9.2 Getting through

Telephone words

1 Match the sentences 1–6 with the sentences A–G which have similar meaning.

0 He's busy.	A Does that suit you?
1 I'll get back to you.	B He's unavailable.
2 I'll put you through.	C Hold on, please.
3 I'll write it down.	D I'll call you back.
4 I'll read that back to you.	E I'll just repeat that.
5 Is that convenient?	F I'll connect you.
6 Wait a moment.	G I'll take it down.

2 Complete each conversation using the words in brackets.

0 **A** Sorry, I can't find the number. Are you in a hurry?

   B No, that's OK. (hold on) I'll hold on for a moment.

1 **A** Have you got his number?

   B One minute. (look up) _____
_____

2 **A** So, his name is Giles Kilkeady K-I-L-K-E-A-D-Y.

   B OK. (read back) _____
_____

3 **A** Can you help me to write this proposal?

   B Sorry. (tied up) _____
_____

4 **A** Is that the end of the meeting?

   B Yes. (run out) _____
_____

5 **A** I can't come to the meeting on Friday. I leave for Spain that day.

   B I see. (bring forward) _____
_____

6 **A** I'm sorry, Mr James' line is engaged at the moment.

   B OK. (call back) _____

7 **A** Can I speak to Colin Spackman, please?

   B One moment. (put through) _____
_____

8 **A** Can you tell her that Fred called?

   B Of course. (pass on) _____
_____

3 Complete this telephone conversation using ONE word in each space.

Davies Hello. I'd like to (0) *speak* to Yuko Sato, please.

Reception One moment. I'll try to (1) _____ you. I'm sorry Ms Sato isn't (2) _____ today. Can I (3) _____ a message?

Davies I have a question about your women's fashion accessories.

Receptionist OK. I'll (4) _____ you though to Sales. Maybe they can help you. Can I just (5) _____ down your name?

Davies Yes, of course. It's Stephanie Davies.

Receptionist One (6) _____, Miss Davies. I'm going to put you on (7) _____ for a moment ... OK, go ahead.

Sales Hello, Sales.

Davies Oh, hello. I'm (8) _____ from an independent ladies' boutique. We're interested in buying some of your fashion accessories.

Sales OK. Well I think the best thing is to arrange an appointment to see Yuko Sato, our regional manager. She's out of the office today. Can you call (9) _____ tomorrow?

Davies Yes. What time would be (10) _____?

Sales Around 9.30 would be best, if that (11) _____ you. Can I just take your name, anyway?

Davies Yes, it's Davies.

Sales OK, Miss Davies, I will (12) _____ the message on that you called.

Davies Thank you.

Correcting and checking

4 Each email below contains six mistakes – one of each type of common error. Find them and correct them.

Dear Rebecca

I ~~still am~~ waiting ∧ *for* an answer to the email I sent you last week. My colleague Erica need to know your answer before she will go to Germany. Please let know me by Wenesday at the latest.

Thanks

Jane

Dear Mr Duncan

Regarding to your order for a Bosch washing machine, I am afraid that this item are not in stock. However, I can offer you the other option, which is too a German-made machine. I attached a full description of the product to this email and I hope it will meet your requirments.

Yours sincerely

Onkar (Sales)

Hello John

I have tried to telephone you yesterday, but I think you were out at the lunch with a client. We are having tomorrow a meeting at 10 o'clock with a brand consultant to discuss about our new marketing campaign. He is a very intresting guy who have worked with some top companies, so please try to come.

Felix

Dear Maria

I got your message in this morning about the interviews which will next week take place. In the answer to your question, I think it will be better if they were group interviews. This will give us the oportunity to see how the different candidates interacts with each other.

Thanks

Jane

9.3 Writing Test: Part Two

1 **Look at the exam question below and the letter one student wrote. Which two recommendations from A–D did the student NOT follow?**

2 **Now, thinking about your answer to exercise 1, rewrite and improve the letter.**

Dear Mr Duffy

Thanks very much for choosing our company. We'd love to have the chance to work with you. What's more, if you could extend the trial period to 12 months, we could offer you another 8 per cent reduction in the price.

Here are the answers to your other points:

– Our normal collection hours are 7am–8pm. There's just a small fee for collection at other times.

– We can cover all the locations mentioned, but it'd be good to know how many cars you expect to hire from each place.

– We can also do chauffeur driven cars.

All in all, I think you can be confident that we'll handle this business professionally and for a good price. Please give me a call to arrange a good time to meet.

Best wishes

Steve

- You work for APIS Car rental, a small but growing car hire business. You have just received this email.
- Read the email and the other information, including the notes you have already written.
- Using all the notes, write a letter in reply to Dave Duffy. (120–140 words.)

To: APIS Car rental
From: Dave Duffy (Purchasing manager)

Further to our meetings with you last week, we would like to discuss the possibility of a 6-month trial contract. Here is a reminder of our requirements:

– 24-hour availability for car collection

– coverage of all our main locations in the UK (London, Birmingham, Manchester, Glasgow, Leeds and Newcastle)

– the option of chauffeur driven cars for senior executives

We expect to make on average about 30–40 car rentals per week and it is vital that we know you are able to manage this quantity.

I look forward to hearing from you.

Handwritten notes:
- Offer discount for 12 months
- Cars can be collected between 7am and 8pm. Extra fee if outside those hours
- Ask for approximate figures for each location
- Prices can vary from one location to another
- Not own depot here, but good partner

Location	Number of cars in fleet
London	50
Birmingham	25
Manchester	30
Glasgow	20
Leeds	10
Newcastle	0

GEORDIE CAR RENTAL

Modern fleet of cars. Flexible hours, fast service, fair rates.

10.1 Management

1 Complete this flow chart showing five steps to success in business using the verbs in the box.

implement   recognise   develop
fill   ~~set out~~   plan   renew

0 *Set out* with a clear vision.

↓

1 _____ an understanding of your market and customers.

↓

2 _____ your weaknesses and _____ the gaps.

↓

3 _____ your strategy and consider how you will _____ it.

↓

4 _____ your offer regularly to respond to changes in the market.

2 Find the opposite of the underlined word. The first letter has been given for you.

0 to <u>take</u> an opportunity: to miss an opportunity

1 to <u>succeed</u>: to f_____

2 It's one of my <u>strengths</u>: It's one of my w_____

3 It was a complete <u>failure</u>: It was a great s_____

4 to be <u>ignorant</u> of trends: to be a_____ of trends

5 a <u>slowly</u> changing market: a r_____ changing market

6 to <u>repeat</u> the same mistakes: to l_____ from your mistakes

3 Replace each underlined word with the correct form of the word.

0 I have <u>attendance</u> a lot of courses. attended

1 The business has developed quite <u>rapid</u>.

2 We have a five-year <u>strategic</u> to grow the business.

3 She doesn't <u>recognition</u> her own weaknesses.

4 We have to increase people's <u>aware</u> of our brand.

5 The road to <u>successful</u> is not an easy one.

6 He is quite <u>weakness</u> at planning.

7 They <u>setting</u> their salesmen very difficult targets.

8 Planning is one thing, <u>implement</u> is another.

4 Read the text about changes in the music industry. In most lines, there is one extra word. Some lines are correct. If a line is correct, write CORRECT next to the line. If there is an extra word, write it in CAPITALS next to the line.

0	In the past, the music industry used to promote a new artists by releasing new albums	A
00	as records or CDs. Nowadays, that has all changed. The record companies are aware	CORRECT
1	of the problem but they don't know how to can solve it. They know that when they	_____
2	invest in an artist, they will not get a return on their investment right away from the profits	_____
3	of the first album. In order so to be profitable, the artist must repeat their success again	_____
4	and again. This is because the costs of producing and advertising have increased so	_____
5	much in recent years. Music companies also recognise that more and more than music	_____
6	is downloaded for free on the Internet. You would think about that the consequences of	_____
7	these factors would be fewer new artists and less original music, because an original means	_____
8	risk. But this is not the case. The Internet has been allowed artists the opportunity to reach	_____
9	to their audience without the help of a record company. In addition, they can develop	_____
10	their audience and, at the same time, earn a reasonable income by touring and playing live.	_____

Conditionals

5 Study the following conditional sentences and decide if the underlined verbs are correct or incorrect. If they are incorrect, replace them with the correct form.

0 What would you do if someone <u>offers</u> you the chance to play in a band? *offered*

1 If you <u>are</u> able to recognise your weaknesses, you will be a better manager.

2 If you don't work hard, you never <u>achieve</u> success.

3 If you <u>would heat</u> water to 100° C, it boils.

4 If I <u>knew</u> the answer, I would tell you.

5 If I <u>didn't meet</u> her, I would have missed this opportunity.

6 You will never achieve much unless you <u>will have</u> great ambition.

7 If I <u>was</u> you, I would think about finding a partner for this venture.

8 If he had learnt from his mistakes, he <u>wouldn't be</u> in this situation now.

9 No company can survive if it just <u>kept</u> on doing the same thing.

10 If you <u>would fail</u>, it wouldn't be the end of the world.

6 Match the two halves of each proverb. Do you have a similar proverb in your language?

0 If you can't beat them,	A she would have been my uncle.
1 If at first you don't succeed,	B we would not enjoy the sun.
2 If something can go wrong,	C try, try and try again.
3 If you can't stand the heat,	D you will please no-one.
4 If you are not part of the solution,	E join them.
5 If there were no clouds	F it will.
6 If you try to please everyone	G then you are part of the problem.
7 If my aunt had been a man	H get out of the kitchen.

7 Read the text and complete the sentences below.

Ed Sheeran is currently one of the most famous musicians in the world. Fans stream his music millions of times, with one track even streamed over a billion times on Spotify™ alone. By early 2017, his videos had collectively been watched over 3.5 billion times on YouTube. Sheeran is also well-known as a clever businessperson who keeps a close eye on the sales figures every time he releases a new song.

Sheeran was born in England and his parents encouraged his interest in music from when he was young. As a child, he joined a choir and developed his singing. He also learnt to play the guitar. When he left school, he studied music at a college for a while but left the music school early to start recording his own songs. Soon, his songs became popular on YouTube and he released his first album without the support of a record company.

In 2010, after playing live in the UK night after night, he decided to go to Los Angeles and try to find success there. He met the actor Jamie Foxx who owned a nightclub. He stayed at Foxx's house and played at his club. Soon, he was becoming popular in the USA as well as in the UK, and he achieved greater fame when he supported Taylor Swift on her world tour.

In the end, Sheeran signed with a record label and now his music sells globally. In 2015, he was listed as the 27th highest earning celebrity in the world.

0 He wouldn't have become a musician if his parents hadn't *encouraged his interest in music.*

1 He wouldn't have developed his singing, if he

_____

2 He wouldn't have started to record his own songs if he _____

3 If he hadn't gone to Los Angeles, he wouldn't

_____

4 If he hadn't supported Taylor Swift, he wouldn't

_____

1 Complete the crossword by adding in the missing words in this conversation about a solution to a problem with a web designer.

A So (**1 across**), the problem is that we have employed a designer who can't do the job. We urgently need to _____ (**1 down**) this problem. There are two things we can do: _____ (**10 down**) possibility is to pay for the work that has been done and find another designer.

B And what's the _____ (**5 across**)?

A The other _____ (**3 down**) is to work with the designer until we can _____ (**8 across**) a design solution we like.

B I'm not so _____ (**15 across**) that he has the competence to deliver what we want.

A But there is _____ (**13 across**) guarantee that another designer can either. What _____ (**2 across**) we do if a new designer was _____ (**12 down**) bad as the first?

B I've got another _____ (**11 across**). Let's employ a consultant to evaluate the current designer. The advantage _____ (**6 down**) that would be that we'd get an expert view.

A I agree. If someone else _____ (**9 down**) an independent evaluation, it'd be more objective.

B On the other _____ (**14 across**), it might be expensive.

A Well, we can _____ (**7 across**) about the cost _____ (**4 down**). The priority is to get the new website finished.

2 In Part Three of the Speaking Test, two candidates are given this question to discuss:

> The company that you work for, an online travel agency selling flights and holidays, would like to promote itself more widely. You have been asked to come up with ideas. Discuss with your partner:
> - how it can do this without greatly increasing its advertising expenditure
> - what kind of promotions it could offer.

Look at their conversation and correct the underlined mistakes.

A The main problem is how (0) promote *to promote* the company without spending a lot on advertising. What do you think?

B Well, one option (1) can be to post reviews of our company on the Internet.

A How would that work?

B Well, if you (2) will find a holiday on the Internet, you generally want to know another (3) person opinion of it. There (4) is a lot of sites where you find personal reviews of holidays. If we (5) was to offer our customers a small payment to write a review of their holiday with us, we could post the good ones on other websites.

A That's (6) good idea. It would have the advantage (7) to being like a word-of-mouth recommendation. I suppose we could even post a (8) little reviews ourselves.

B I'm not sure that (9) will be legal. Let's start (10) on trying to get customers (11) writing reviews. And what (12) are you think about promotions?

A One solution is to offer loyalty points, (13) in order that customers can get a discount the second or third time that they book.

B I like that idea. I think it works (14) good for a lot of travel companies.

Managing a project

3 Complete the conversation about a project to construct a stage for a concert by putting ONE preposition in each space.

A How's everything going with the stage construction project? Are you (0) *on* schedule?

B Actually, we're (1) _____ of schedule. We will finish on 2nd July, well (2) _____ time for sound testing on the 6th.

A And have you kept (3) _____ the budget?

B More or less. The scaffolders quoted £26,000 and their final bill is £28,000, so we're a little (4) _____ budget there.

A And did you manage to get the new LED screen?

B No, we ran (5) _____ of time there. The manufacturers were three weeks (6) _____ schedule, so we cancelled the order. We've used a traditional LCD. I think it'll work fine.

4 Match each expression on the left with the one closest in meaning on the right.

1 following	A so
2 because of	B further to
3 therefore	C in order to
4 so that	D as a result of

5 Use the best expression from exercise 4 to complete each of these sentences.

0 *Because of* a misunderstanding with our shipping department, your order has been delayed.

1 _____ the decision of the board to be more environmentally active, the company will no longer use plastic packaging.

2 _____ speed things up, I've passed your request straight to the Director.

3 Your contract has now expired. _____ unless you renew it, we cannot send you any more issues of the magazine.

6 Write the notes in emails 1–4 as full sentences.

1
To: All staff
From: Jean Fevre
Subject: New venue and date for training course

Because / high demand / training course next week / we / decided / move it / a larger venue. The course / now take place / Marriot Hotel / 4 March.

Because of the high demand for the training course next week _____
_____
_____

2
To: IT Director
From: 'Concerto' Project manager
Subject: Delays

Unfortunately / we / experience / few problems / new software. This / due / programming fault. We / try / correct it / and with luck it / work again / tomorrow afternoon / the latest.

_____
_____
_____

3
To: Gabriella Santos
From: Dean Taylor
Subject: Help with proposal

Further / our meeting last week / I / work / proposal / our new Chinese partner. However, it / not be ready / time for our next meeting. I / attach / this email. Could you / look / it and tell / how can / improve?

_____
_____
_____

4
To: All departments
From: Cost control manager
Subject: Office stationery

I / still wait / response / my request of 12 September concerning purchases / office stationery. I need this information / order / prepare the budgets / next year.
Please send / information / soon / possible. I run / time.

_____
_____
_____

1 In the Listening Test Part Three, you should always look closely at the multiple choice options before you listen to the passage. Some answers are more likely than others. Look at the choices and underline the most UNLIKELY answer to each question.

• You will hear an interview with a management consultant, Gerry Roberts, explaining how to relieve stress.

1 The secret to feeling less stressed is
   A changing your habits in a few small ways.
   B a big mystery.
   C to stop worrying.

2 When you make a day list, you must
   A include all the things that you have to do.
   B be realistic about what you can do in a day.
   C be sure to put the items in order of importance.

3 If you have to write a 10,000 word report, you should write on your day list:
   A leave until another day.
   B write the report.
   C write part of the report.

4 If you take breaks in the day, try to
   A keep them short.
   B use the time to do some personal jobs.
   C get some exercise.

5 Taking breaks can make you
   A feel more relaxed.
   B feel tired.
   C work better.

6 When accepting work from others, don't
   A agree without considering first what you can do.
   B agree to any deadlines.
   C be afraid to say no.

7 The interviewer always arrives a little early at work so that he can
   A read a magazine or newspaper.
   B deal with any emergencies.
   C get home earlier at the end of the day.

8 Chatting to colleagues
   A wastes the company's time.
   B can give you good ideas.
   C helps you to worry less about work problems.

---

2 Now read the transcript of the test and circle the correct answer to each question.

Interviewer So, Gerry Roberts is here to give some tips on how we can feel less stressed at work and manage our time better. You're looking very relaxed, Gerry. What's the secret?

Gerry Roberts There's no great secret to it. A lot of what I say will seem obvious. It's just a question of making a few simple changes to your lifestyle.

Interviewer For example?

Gerry Roberts Well, the first thing you need to do is stop worrying about all the things you have to do. The best way to do this is to make a short list of what you hope to achieve the following day. Make sure that they are achievable – so don't put down 'write report', which happens to be 10,000 words long. Instead, put down 'write 500 words of report'.
The second thing is to make sure that you give yourself proper breaks during the day. This is particularly important if you work in front of a computer all day. Ideally these breaks will include some exercise, like going for a short walk or a swim. You'll be amazed, if you do this, how much better you feel when you return to your work. It will actually make you more productive.

Interviewer And a lot of people feel stressed because others are depending on them to finish a piece of work, for example. How can you deal with this?

Gerry Roberts It's very important when you are accepting work from others to be realistic about what you can do in the time you have. So always think about what is possible and don't just say 'Yes, of course I'll do it' to please them. Think about what is realistic and don't promise to do more than that.

Interviewer One thing I do when I get to work is to arrive a little early so that I can deal with any unexpected problems before I start work. If there aren't any, I just spend 15 minutes reading the paper.

Gerry Roberts I think that's an excellent idea. It also gives you the chance to chat to people about things other than work. Thinking only about work from the moment you arrive at the office to the moment you leave isn't healthy. It makes you feel alone and under pressure. It really helps to talk about your problems or concerns with a colleague, even if there is not much they can do about it.

11.1   Ethical economics

Financial and trade terms

1 Match the trade and financial terms to the correct definition.

> export costs   a commodity   overheads
> GDP   break-even   freight   ~~a middleman~~
> markup   market price

0 *a middleman*: someone who buys a product from one person and sells it on to another

1 _____: the total value of goods produced and sold by a country in a year

2 _____: the point at which sales equal costs

3 _____: fixed costs like rent, electricity, heating

4 _____: goods transported over long distances by land, air or sea

5 _____: the difference between the buying price and the selling price

6 _____: a commonly traded basic product like coffee, aluminium, oranges

7 _____: expenses involved in transporting goods to another country (such as taxes, insurance)

8 _____: the standard price for a product or service

2 Write the missing letters to complete the spider chart showing different types of cost.

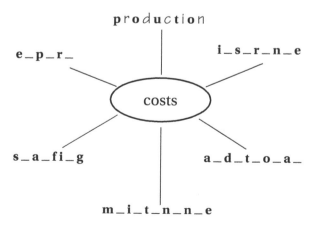

p r o d u c t i o n

e _ p _ r _   i _ s _ r _ n _ e

costs

s _ a _ f i _ g   a _ d _ t _ o _ a _

m _ i _ t _ n _ e

3 Complete the sentences describing the process of exporting coffee with the past participle form of the verb in brackets.

0 Coffee is *grown* (grow) all over the world.

1 Coffee farm labourers are _____ (pay) very low wages.

2 Most of the coffee is _____ (export) to the developed world.

3 It is _____ (transport) by ship.

4 Some is _____ (buy) directly from the producer.

5 It is usually _____ (package) by the retailer.

6 It is _____ (sell) with a high markup.

4 Use the expressions of quantity in the box to complete the sentences.

> ~~roughly~~   average   tiny   excessive
> small   increasing   minimum   least

0 GB £1 is *roughly* equivalent to US $1.2.

1 On _____ a British person drinks six cups of tea a day.

2 The typical coffee producer only gets a _____ proportion of the final selling price: about 4 per cent.

3 Fairtrade is not perfect, but it's a _____ step in the right direction.

4 An _____ number of coffee shops are selling Fairtrade products.

5 £5 for a cup of coffee is _____.

6 A lot of governments in western countries have fixed a _____ wage to protect the lowest paid workers.

7 I try to give money to charity at _____ once a month.

Articles

5 Each of the following sentences contains ONE mistake with the use of *the, a, an, some* or the zero article. Correct them.

0 I hope to see her at the Frankfurt Book Fair the next week. *Book Fair ~~the~~ next week*

1 Can you book me the taxi to the station, please?

2 I have an information that I think will interest you.

3 Saudi Aramco is a biggest oil company in the world.

4 I'm sorry to be late. A train was delayed by an hour.

5 There has been the enormous increase in the number of people going to university.

6 I never get much time to read a newspaper at the work.

7 Can we meet in Red Lion pub at around 6 o'clock?

8 It's very bad situation.

9 In last five years, the company has increased its sales by 60 per cent.

10 Do you have the paper I could write your address on?

6 Complete the sentences using *the* or 0 (the zero article) in each gap.

0 We are going on holiday to Greece in *the* summer.

1 I work at _____ night and sleep in _____ day.

2 We are based in _____ Germany but we operate all over _____ world.

3 In _____ last ten years, we have taken on _____ 40 new employees.

4 _____ United Nations was founded in 1945 after _____ Second World War.

5 I need to be at _____ home in time for _____ supper.

6 Will you go to _____ university next year?

7 My son is studying at _____ University of California.

Pronunciation

7 In the word *average* there seem to be three syllables, AV-ER-AGE. In fact there are only two, AV-RAGE. The middle syllable has been compressed. Look at these other words with compressed syllables and underline the syllable that is NOT pronounced.

vulnerable	comfortable	medicine
secretary	ordinary	difference
interested	business	valuable
withdrawal		

8 These sentences about the history of the Fairtrade movement contain some common grammatical mistakes. Sometimes the wrong word is used, sometimes a word is missing, sometimes the word order is wrong. Correct each underlined mistake.

0 The Fairtrade Foundation has been operating <u>since</u> over 25 years. *for*

1 In 1992 the price of coffee fell by half in just a <u>little</u> months.

2 This was _____ big disaster for many coffee-producing countries.

3 These countries' economies depended <u>for</u> coffee for their income.

4 The Fairtrade Foundation teaches farmers how _____ compete in international markets.

5 They also discuss <u>about</u> global trade issues with national governments.

6 They have been doing this for the <u>ten past</u> years.

7 They <u>must to</u> convince people that Fairtrade is good for free trade.

8 If you increase trade, the money doesn't <u>necessary</u> go to the people at the bottom of the chain.

9 You have to persuade people <u>operating</u> with each other more fairly.

10 Consumers are realising that they should buy products that <u>do</u> a difference to people's lives.

11 <u>Meet</u> the farmers and farm-workers and <u>see</u> the conditions they live in can have a big effect on your attitude.

11.2 Discussing trends

Describing trends

1 Write the opposite of each phrase.

0 to go up: to go down

1 to increase: to d_____

2 to rise: to f_____

3 to crash: to s_____

4 to reach a low point: to reach a p_____

5 to fluctuate: to r_____ s_____

2 Study the graph from *Inforse Europe*, which shows how energy could be used in a sustainable way over 40 years. Then, using the verbs below, complete the text describing the trends which the graph shows.

| fall | ~~reduce~~ increase remain level out |

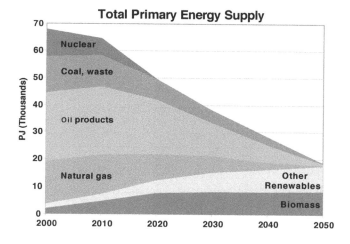

The graph shows how we can (0) *reduce* our dependence on fuels like oil and gas over 40 years. In order to do this the total amount of energy supplied will have to (1) _____ from 68,000 to 19,000 PJ by 2050. The use of Biomass will (2) _____ to 5,000 PJ by 2020 and then (3) _____ after that. At the same time, the use of other renewable forms of energy will not (4) _____ stable, but continue to rise up to 2050.

3 Read the text below about the future of nuclear energy. Choose the best word to fill each gap from A, B, C or D.

Nuclear power is once again back on the (0) A. For years, particularly following the Chernobyl disaster, it was not diplomatic for politicians to talk about the nuclear (1) _____. So what has changed? There are three factors.

First, the (2) _____ in global warming has resulted in all governments wanting to take action to (3) _____ carbon dioxide emissions. Burning nuclear fuel does not produce any CO_2. Secondly, (4) _____ there have been many efforts to look for alternative clean energy sources, (5) _____ to now these have made only a small contribution to our energy needs. Lastly, demand for energy, especially electricity, is still rising and is expected to reach a (6) _____ in 2020. This is because the (7) _____ of new technology used in the home – computers, home entertainment systems – is also increasing.

At the same time, energy supply is (8) _____, as old power stations close down. In other words, we need to build powerful new facilities to fill the (9) _____. Nuclear has many advantages and only one disadvantage, which is how to deal with the waste. But with the new, more (10) _____ generation of nuclear power stations, this problem is also declining.

0	A agenda	B headlines	C point	D track
1	A choose	B option	C power	D one
2	A rising	B rise	C rose	D risen
3	A decline	B reduction	C reduce	D fall
4	A however	B although	C but	D yet
5	A in	B off	C up	D back
6	A finish	B summit	C increase	D peak
7	A number	B amount	C progress	D lot
8	A reduction	B decline	C falling	D down
9	A missing	B land	C gap	D form
10	A efficient	B increasing	C industry	D good

A proposal

4 Match the two halves of each phrase used in writing a proposal.

0	Thank you	A	I would like to point out that …
1	Please don't hesitate to contact me	B	of using a hotel would be …
2	The advantage	C	for your letter regarding …
3	One other thing	D	are as follows:
4	Before I give more details	E	I would recommend that …
5	We would be delighted	F	to work with you.
6	The main elements of our proposal	G	if you would like to discuss any of these points.
7	In order to keep the overall cost down	H	we should consider is …

5 Which sections of a proposal letter do the sentences in exercise 4 belong to? Complete the table.

Introducing a proposal	Thank you for your letter regarding …
Comparing pros and cons	
Balancing and concluding	

6 You work for a company that organises corporate events. Read the letter from a prospective customer in answer to your advertisement and, using the notes, complete the proposal letter below.

Dear Ms Harrison

I saw your advertisement in the Evening Post and was very interested in your services.

a dinner with a comedian and a dance band

We would like to organise an event for about 200 staff and key customers. I was thinking of a dinner with some light entertainment. Because of the large number of people I imagine it would have to take place at a conference centre, but you may have another suggestion.

Please can you send me a proposal with an approximate idea of the cost.

Many thanks.

Yours sincerely

Derek Cook

Churchill Hotel banquet hall £40 per head approx (Bar drinks not included)

CORPORATE ENTERTAINMENT AND EVENTS

We specialise in organising corporate and customer events, such as

- team building activities
- themed parties
- guest speakers
- formal dinners

Contact Katie Harrison for further details.

Dear Mr Cook

Thank you for _____

We would be delighted to _____

Before I give more details, _____

The main elements of our proposal are as follows:

_____

The advantage of using a hotel would be that _____

_____

One other thing we should consider is _____

_____

As to the cost, _____

_____

In order to keep the overall cost down, I would

recommend that _____

Please don't hesitate to _____

I look forward to _____

Yours sincerely

11.3 Reading Test: Part Three

Do Part Three of the Reading Test. Give yourself 12 minutes to complete the task.

- Read the article below about the economist, Adam Smith, and the questions that follow it.
- For each question (1–6), choose the best answer (A, B, C or D).

Adam Smith, the father of free trade and author of the free trader's bible, *The Wealth of Nations*, has been honoured twice. Firstly, his face appears on £20 notes printed by the Bank of England from 2007–2020. And secondly, he is the subject of a book published by the American satirist PJ O'Rourke in a series called 'Books that Changed the World'.

So what did Adam Smith stand for exactly? Even though he wrote in the 18th century, many of his observations about the economy are true today. His basic theory was that if you give people the freedom to improve their own economic situation, they will also improve everyone else's: *'It is not from the benevolence of the butcher, the brewer, or the baker that we expect our dinner, but from their regard to their own interest.'*

Writing at the time of the industrial revolution and the beginning of manufacturing, he also recognised the importance of dividing work into specialised tasks. In other words, if each person concentrated on a task they were good at, the total effort would be more productive. This lesson has now been adopted on a global scale. In each developed or developing country goods are imported from other countries where they are produced most cheaply and efficiently. In this way free trade becomes the natural way to improve standards of living all over the world.

O'Rourke agrees that Smith's ideas are still relevant to us, but not because of economics. He disagrees with people who think that there is something immoral in believing in the individual's right to promote his own profit and self-interest.

'His importance was not just to economics, it was the connection of morality to economics,' says O'Rourke. 'That was his true genius.'

Smith believed that people were motivated by more than profit; they also wanted to please other people and to win their approval. By what he called 'self-command' people are able to control selfish feelings and do 'benevolent acts', that is to show kindness and charity towards others.

O'Rourke thinks that Adam Smith's important economic message is for governments. The less that they interfere in the economy, the better it does. 'Economics is forever telling us to leave people alone,' he says. The trouble, he thinks, is that governments are always trying to regulate business and economic activity in order to justify their own existence.

1 The title of Adam Smith's book is
   A *Books that Changed the World*
   B *The Wealth of Nations*
   C *The Free Trader's Bible*
   D *The Bank of England*

2 Adam Smith believed that people
   A are basically selfish.
   B value freedom more than anything else.
   C help each other by helping themselves.
   D want to improve their neighbour's standard of living.

3 If work is divided into specialised tasks
   A it creates more employment.
   B it makes goods more expensive.
   C you can make more specialised products.
   D you can produce more.

4 The principle of free trade will
   A make everyone in the world richer.
   B help to make goods cheaper.
   C be adopted in under-developed countries.
   D not improve the quality of goods.

5 Smith also believed that people naturally wanted to
   A be kind to others.
   B control others.
   C work harder than others.
   D educate themselves.

6 O'Rourke thinks that governments should
   A regulate businesses more strictly.
   B interfere when they have to.
   C allow businesses to get on with what they want to do.
   D be more concerned with economics.

12.1 Business law

Legal terms

1 Complete the phrases describing ways to complain about someone's behaviour through the law courts.

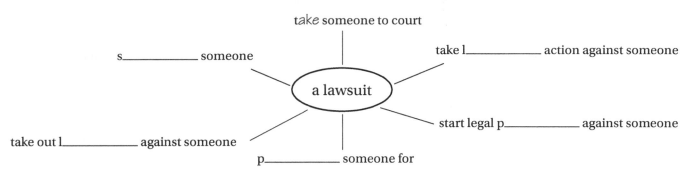

take someone to court

s_____ someone

take l_____ action against someone

a lawsuit

start legal p_____ against someone

take out l_____ against someone

p_____ someone for

---

2 Complete the sentences using the words below.

> rights court sue prosecute case copyright trademark litigation defence ~~judge~~ compensation

0 The judge ruled that Galacall should pay $400,000 in damages to the rival company.

1 In 2007 Viacom announced that it was taking Google™ to _____ to protect its material being published on the website YouTube.

2 It said that Google's use of the material was a breach of _____.

3 Other companies also said they would _____ Google if it did not remove their material.

4 Google's _____ was that users, not the company itself, put this material into a public space.

5 The roaring lion is the _____ of MGM film productions.

6 In 1985 Michael Jackson bought the _____ to all the Beatles songs for US $47.5 million.

7 An interesting recent _____ involved the State of California and various car companies.

8 The state of California wants to _____ the car companies for unnecessarily polluting the atmosphere.

9 It said that it wanted _____ for the costs that would result from the effect on the climate.

10 In response the Automobile Manufacturers Alliance has taken out _____ against the state of California to block its environmental laws.

---

3 Complete the article by choosing the best sentence (A–G) for each gap (1–6).

It is a fact that America is the most litigious society in the world. (0) D. The successful action brought by Stella Liebeck against McDonald's over a spilled cup of coffee is a well-known example. But was her case in fact so unreasonable? (1) _____

On February 27, 1992, 79-year-old Stella Liebeck stopped for breakfast at a McDonald's drive-through restaurant. (2) _____ But as she pulled the lid off the coffee cup, boiling hot coffee (around 80°C) spilled onto her lap. It burnt her legs, leaving lasting damage. She was immobile for several months afterwards and her daughter gave up work to look after her.

She hired lawyer Reed Morgan, who demanded $100,000 in compensation, and $300,000 as a punishment. (3) _____

During the trial it was discovered that McDonald's sold its coffee at 80°C, at least 20°C above the industry standard. (4) _____ What's more, McDonald's had known about the burn risk for over ten years, because other people had also sued the company. In spite of this, Stella was found by the jury to be 20 per cent responsible for the accident. (5) _____

She was awarded $160,000 in damages for her medical costs and disability. (6) _____ More hurtful to her was the fact that her case became used as an example of how people blame others for accidents which are really their own fault.

A She lived the rest of her life in pain and discomfort.

B McDonald's refused to settle out of court and the trial took place in 1994.

C This is actually what happened.

D People are ready to take an employer or a retailer to court over the smallest thing.

E If the coffee that spilled onto Stella had been 5°C cooler, it would not have burnt her so seriously.

F When she had got her breakfast, she stopped the car to put cream into her coffee.

G Because of this the amount of compensation she received was reduced.

Indirect questions and tags

4 Put these questions in the correct order.

0 it / isn't / nice day, / a / it's / ?

It's a nice day, isn't it?

1 French, / aren't / you're / you / ?

You're _____

2 are / sue / they / to / going / you / think / do / ?

Do you _____

3 what / is / know / about / you / do / this / ?

Do you _____

4 wondering / was / you / I / help / if / me / could / ?

I was _____

5 when / have / do / register / I / to / you / know / ?

Do you _____

6 charge / tell / who / can / in / is / you / me / ?

Can you _____

7 I'd / know / she / to / left / why / like

I'd like _____

8 offers, / you're / to / open / new / you / aren't ?

You're _____

9 can / works / how / explain / it / you / ?

Can you _____

10 long / have / I'd / here / how / like / worked / you / to know

I'd like _____

5 Convert each direct question into an indirect question using the words given.

0 What time is it?

Can you tell me what time it is?

1 What do you think?

I'd like to know _____

2 How much does it cost?

Could you tell me _____

3 Is it legal?

Do you think _____

4 How long would it take?

I was wondering _____

5 What exactly did they complain about?

Can you tell me _____

6 Do they own the rights to the name?

I wonder _____

7 Which firm did you use?

Do you remember _____

6 Convert each direct question into a tag question.

0 Do you come from China?

You come from China, don't you?

1 Didn't we meet at the Berlin conference?

We met _____?

2 Is Li your first name?

Li is _____?

3 Hasn't the meeting been postponed?

The meeting _____?

4 Do you take sugar in your coffee?

You take _____?

5 Am I late?

I'm not _____?

6 Don't they own the rights to the name?

They own _____?

7 Doesn't he work for ABC?

He works _____?

Pronunciation

7 Long vowel /iː/ and short vowel /e/. When the letter *e* appears between two consonants it is sometimes pronounced /iː/ as in *been* and sometimes /e/ as in *get*. Decide how to pronounce the underlined *e* in the following words and complete the table.

media legal level recent metal secret
previous detail precious separate decade
retail creditor medium female pressure

/iː/	/e/
media	

12.2 Handling questions

1 Complete the following phrases for responding to questions using the verbs in the box.

repeat come back get back follow catch thank is mean answer ~~check~~ mind

0 I just need to *check* with someone first.

1 Sorry. I don't _____ you.

2 I'm afraid I'm unable to _____ that at the moment.

3 I'll _____ to that point later on.

4 Can you explain what you _____ exactly?

5 Let me _____ to you on that.

6 Do you _____ if I answer that at the end?

7 Sorry, can you _____ the question?

8 _____ you for asking that.

9 Sorry. I didn't _____ that.

10 That _____ a good question.

2 During a presentation you are giving, you get various questions. Choose an appropriate response from exercise 1 to use in each situation.

0 Someone asks a question which you think you understand, but you are not completely sure.
Can you explain what you mean exactly?

1 Someone at the back of the room asks you a question, but you cannot hear what they say.
_____

2 Someone asks you a question, but you don't have with you the information you need to answer it.
_____

3 Someone asks you a question which addresses the main point you have been discussing.
_____

4 Someone interrupts your presentation to ask about something which you are going to explain later in your talk.
_____

5 Someone asks you a question which you don't understand because it is too complicated and technical.
_____

3 Read the advice about how to handle questions. Match the correct headings (A–F) with each paragraph (1–4). There is one extra heading.

(0) E
Before your presentation, make a list of the questions that you might be asked. Give the list to a colleague and ask them to fire the questions at you. Keep some material in reserve so that if you are asked a question, you can present this new information as if it was spontaneous.

(1) _____
When you have finished your presentation, don't say immediately 'Any questions?' Instead, take a couple of minutes' break and then begin to take questions. If there still aren't any, suggest some yourself: for example, 'I'm often asked … .' This will encourage the audience to start asking questions.

(2) _____
It's very important to engage with the person who is asking the question, so try to maintain eye contact with them and to listen carefully to what they have to say. This is respectful and will help to prevent any conflict during the session.

(3) _____
It's very easy to allow a questioner to take you into an area which is not necessarily relevant to the main point of your talk. Always keep in mind the main objective of your presentation and return to it as many times as possible. Respond to every question, even if you don't think it is relevant, but keep your answer short.

(4) _____
Make sure that you and not the audience have the last word. Give a short summary or make an appeal to the audience for action, or at least for agreement. Remember that the audience's attention is greatest at the beginning and at the end of the session.

A Give your audience time to think

B Don't be distracted

C Focus on the questioner

D Finish strongly

E Prepare well

F Ignore irrelevant questions

Writing a press release

4 Read the press releases A–C. Correct the underlined mistakes.

A

To mark their 50th anniversary, Goodwins Ice Cream is holding a competition (0) <u>for</u> *to* find the most interesting new flavour. The winning suggestion will be (1) <u>make</u> into our special anniversary ice cream. The winner will also receive five litres of the ice cream in (2) <u>the</u> special presentation pack. Existing customers and members of the public are invited to submit their suggestions (3) <u>until</u> 31 May.
For more (4) <u>of</u> details visit Goodwin's website at www.goodwinsicecream.com

B

In recent years there (5) <u>was</u> a lot of concern about the use of chemicals in the manufacture of foods. Eat4health has a policy of (6) <u>use</u> only natural preservatives and flavourings in its range of food products. Company spokesman, Gerry Chambers says, 'There's (7) <u>anything</u> wrong with trying to preserve foods and make them last (8) <u>more</u> longer. People have been doing it for thousands of years. We have researched methods that were used in the pre-industrial era and are re-introducing (9) <u>this</u> into our manufacturing processes.'

C

We are pleased to announce that we will soon be opening a new office in Guang Zhou (10) <u>like</u> part of our programme (11) <u>expanding</u> the company's interests in China. The new office will handle operations in Southern China and we are really looking forward (12) <u>for</u> giving local and international businesses the chance to benefit (13) <u>to</u> our real estate expertise.

5 Read the press releases again and say which one is written in the wrong style for a press release. Explain why.

6 You work in the public relations department of Sestro, a company that manages urban transport projects. Read the memo from your colleague and then, using the notes below, write a short press release.

INTERNAL MEMO

Good news. We won the Liverpool tram project to build a single tram line from the centre of the city to Birkenhead. As you know, our offer included the building of a youth community centre and small skateboard park near the main tram terminus. Can you write a press release highlighting this?

Thanks

Fenella

- contract awarded by Liverpoool City Council
- value of contract £16.5 million
- skateboard park and community youth centre will benefit young people in the area
- work to start in January next year

Pronunciation

7 When the letter *u* produces the sound /uː/, in some words the sound /j/ comes before the /uː/. For example *tune* is pronounced: /tjuːn/. Underline the words which have the same /juː/ sound.

future	opportunity	suit
true	produce	music
value	pollute	due
unusual	rude	include

12.3 Speaking Test: Part Three

1 This discussion from Part Three of the Speaking Test is about the best way to recruit a new sales manager. Read the dialogue and say if you think the underlined answers of each candidate A and B are: too formal, too informal, too long or too short.

Examiner So, what do you think is the best way to find a person to replace Kevin, who was very experienced and very good at this job?

Candidate A (0) <u>I am of the opinion that we ought to</u> employ a headhunting agency. *too formal*

Examiner What do you think of that idea, Carlos?

Candidate B (1) <u>Explain, please.</u>

Examiner He said that we should use a headhunter.

Candidate B (2) <u>No, that's wrong.</u> We just need to advertise.

Examiner I think if we want to choose from a bigger range of candidates, advertising is a good solution.

Candidate A I am sorry. (3) <u>I do not properly understand your line of argument</u>.

Examiner What I mean is that we would probably then get a range of older and younger candidates.

Candidate B (4) <u>So what?</u>

Examiner Well, on the one hand someone younger could bring a lot of enthusiasm to the job.

Candidate A (5) <u>Conversely</u>, an older candidate would have more experience.

Candidate B (6) <u>Yeah, definitely.</u>

Examiner So, we really need to decide what kind of person we are looking for before we choose the method of recruitment.

Candidate A (7) <u>And what is your opinion on this</u>?

Examiner I think the job is too important for someone inexperienced, so using a headhunter is the best way.

Candidate A (8) <u>I fully appreciate your point, but to my way of thinking</u> headhunters can be unreliable. Don't you think so?

Candidate B (9) <u>Sorry?</u>

2 Replace each of the underlined phrases (1–9) in exercise 1 with one of the phrases (A–J).

0 D I think we should

A On the other hand,

B I agree with you completely.

C Sorry, could you repeat that?

D I think we should

E Can you explain what you mean exactly?

F I see your point, but for me

G I don't quite follow you.

H What do you think?

I I'm afraid I disagree.

J And what would be the advantage of that?

3 In each of these statements by candidates in Part Three of the Speaking Test, there is one underlined vocabulary mistake. Correct it.

0 The delegates will want to have some free time for <u>their own</u>. *themselves*

1 We should be able to get a <u>decrease</u> on the price of the hotel rooms.

2 On <u>another</u> hand, using a celebrity to endorse the product could be very expensive.

3 I think the most <u>affected</u> way to advertise is on TV.

4 In addition to a good salary, we can offer other benefits <u>as</u> a company car.

5 If we ask employees to reuse paper more, we will <u>win</u> a lot of money.

6 A lot of employees <u>go</u> to work here in their cars every day.

7 I don't think people are <u>interesting</u> in this kind of course.

8 I think we should encourage employees to <u>make</u> more online training courses.

Answer key

MODULE 1

1.1
Ways of working

1 1 flexible 2 permanent 3 full-time 4 employee 5 freelance

2 1 for / at 2 on 3 in 4 round / over 5 to 6 on 7 by 8 from 9 to 10 off 11 with 12 at

3
1 a five-days week
2 ~~since~~ **for** a couple of months
3 ~~few~~ **a few** extra hours
4 I am not ~~every day~~ in the office **every day**.
5 I miss ~~to chat~~ **chatting** to my colleagues.

4
1 /wɜːk/ as in *were* and /wɔːk / as in *fork*
2 /tiːm/ as in *seem* and /taɪm/ as in *I'm*
3 /liːv/ as in *see* and /lɪv/ as in *sit*
4 /tʃaɪld/ as in *cry* and /tʃɪldrən/ as in *fill*
5 /ʃeə/ as in *she* and /tʃeə/ as in *child*

5
1 have been doing
2 have had
3 have known
4 have not been listening
5 have been worrying
6 has been
7 have been thinking
8 has been

6 **Suggested answer:**
You have been working long hours. But have you been spending the extra time productively? Working longer hours doesn't necessarily mean that you are being more productive.

7 **Suggested answers:**
1 check my emails. (present simple)
2 leave work (present simple)
3 am cycling. (present continuous)
4 have a sandwich and a short walk. (present simple)
5 is doing a training course (present continuous)
6 go for a drink with a few colleagues. (present simple)
7 am trying to work. (present continuous)
8 make mistakes with my tenses. (present simple)

8 **Suggested answers:**
1 I've been studying English since I was nine years old.
2 I've been working for Bayer for 18 months.
3 I've only had my new mobile phone for three weeks.
4 I've known that I want to have my own business since I was 16.
5 I've been doing these exercises for about half an hour.

1.2
Making contacts

1 1 specialise 2 of 3 deal 4 report, in 5 for

2
A	Legal advisor	1
B	Head of Sustainable Development	4
C	Personal assistant	0
D	Production foreman	2
E	Press officer	3
F	Car mechanic	5

3
1 Recruitment of staff at all levels
2 Training, career development
3 The HR manager
4 Conferences and job fairs
5 Knowledge of the advertising industry

4
Barney: Hello, Sara, good to see you again. Can I introduce you to Su Li?
Sara: **How do you do,** Su Li? I'm Sara.
Su Li: It's a pleasure. Please call me Su.
Sara: **I am pleased to meet you**, too. Barney has told me about you. **How long have you been here?**
Su Li: I arrived in London two days ago.
Sara: **And is this your first time** in England?
Su Li: Yes, it is.
Sara: **How do you like it**?
Su Li: London is great, but rather expensive.
Sara: Well, **can I join you** two for a coffee?
Su Li: Yes, sure. Are you enjoying the conference?
Sara: Yes, it has been very useful. I **have made** a lot of new contacts. And you?
Su Li: Yes, it's new for me, but I have learnt a lot.
Sara: You work for Taylor Associates, **don't you**?
Su Li: Yes, I am their Chinese agent. And you are with Featherstone, I think.
Sara: Yes, **that's right**.

5 A David should write back or call suggesting a time to meet for a drink

B Ms Kowlowski doesn't need to reply (unless the item doesn't arrive!)

Suggested answer:

Hi Kate

Thanks for your message. I wasn't too surprised about the job either. I'd love to go for a drink. How about 6 o'clock next Wednesday at the Red Lion?

David

6 1 I am writing to inform you that we have received your order and it should arrive shortly.

2 I apologise for sending an incorrect invoice. I am now attaching the correct version.

3 Further to our meeting earlier in the week, please find attached the information you requested.

7 1 I'm sorry but I can't come to the meeting this afternoon. Please let me know what happens.

2 How about meeting at the restaurant? The bad news is that I only have an hour.

3 Good to see you last week and I hope to see you again soon.

8 **Suggested answer:**

Dear Mr Johnstone

I represent Luca Lighting, a company which specialises in high-quality lighting products.

I will be visiting your area next month and would be pleased to have the opportunity to demonstrate our range to you.

Please suggest a time that is convenient to you.

I look forward to hearing from you.

Yours sincerely

1.3
Speaking Test: Part One

1 1 And **what** do you do?

2 **How long** have you been studying?

3 **Do** you have a job lined up afterwards?

4 **What kind of** company is it?

5 And **what** will your job **involve**?

6 And **how** do you feel **about** working for your father?

2 1 hobbies 2 ambitions 3 company's activity

4 job prospects 5 your opinion

4 **Suggested answers:**

1 Yes, I've been working for a company called Lacreal for the last six months.

2 At the moment I'm just working as a trainee in the sales department.

3 Yes, we manufacture and sell a range of cosmetic products.

4 We mainly sell to big department stores and pharmacies.

5 Not at the moment, but I hope to in the future.

6 Sorry, could you repeat the question?

7 I know a lot of people disagree with it, but I really have a problem with it, actually.

8 My ambition is to be an international sales manager and to work abroad.

MODULE 2
2.1
Company benefits

1 1 company 2 flexible 3 promotion 4 pension

5 unpaid 6 holiday 7 off

2 1 care 2 on 3 break 4 pinch 5 place

3 1 E 2 A 3 D 4 C 5 G 6 F

4 1 joined

2 (correct)

3 have been working

4 have you been doing

5 (correct)

6 have taken

7 have developed

8 (correct)

9 moved

10 have been looking

5 **Suggested answer:**

Reynard Inc is based in Birmingham in the UK. The company was first set up in 1906 to make bicycles and motorcycles. It has over 50 years' experience in the manufacture of motorcyles. Today, its main products are bicycles and motorcyles. The company has a subsidiary in the United States, and one in Hungary which opened last year. Recently, it has agreed a new partnership with a Chinese factory.

6 I think we all recognise that incentives are important, // but why? // And what kind of incentives work best? // Should they be financial // or should we concentrate on praising employees for good work // or for achieving their targets? // The answer is not simple // because not every individual responds in the same way.

7

Long 'i' /aɪ/	Short 'i' /ɪ/
recognise	incentive
finance	promise
outline	individual
final	policy
behind	flexible
describe	benefit
	article
	division

2.2
Presenting a company

1　1 C　2 A　3 D　4 B　5 A　6 D

2
1 sixty per cent
2 nineteen-oh-five
3 two thousand and eight
4 five million
5 three thousand two hundred and ten
6 (a) half
7 eleven over four
8 thirty-three point three per cent

3　1 tell　2 brief　3 happy　4 all　5 out　6 show
7 gives　8 coming / listening

4　**Suggested answers:**
1 I'd like to begin by **telling you something about our product**.
2 At this point I will quote our CEO: **having a great product is not enough**.
3 Let's move on **to look at sales / the sales figures**.
4 This chart **shows the turnover for 2017**.
5 Let's take a look **at our profits for last year**.
6 That brings me **to the end of my presentation**.

5
1 Graham Pole reports to John Simmons.
2 Graham has missed work on 22 days.
3 John Simmons suggests that Graham should come to discuss any problems with him.
4 Graham should see John Simmons to explain his situation.

6　From: Sarah Kandarthi
Subject: Suggestions for ~~the~~ staff party
Just a ~~quickly~~ reminder that the staff party will be ~~at~~ **on** 5 December. We have not ~~done~~ **made** a final decision on where it will take place, so please ~~to~~ send me your suggestions. If anyone is not able ~~attending~~ **to attend**, please ~~make~~ **let** me know before ~~the~~ next Friday.

7　1 As a result　2 you hear from me
3 For further information　4 Further to　5 because of
6 If you would like　7 I'd like to point out

2.3
Reading Test: Part One

1　B

2　**Suggested answers:**
A A make of chocolate is now being marketed which can help people feel less stressed.
B This product is one of a range now being marketed on the basis that it will help change your mood rather than giving physical benefits.
C Omega-3 is another product which benefits mental well-being.
D Food experts are advising caution and warning that all the things we eat are important.

3
1 D (*everything you eat is important*)
2 A (*It is every marketer's dream. To take a product which people like …*)
3 B (*With this new range, the focus is much more on food that will help to change your mood.*)
4 A (*can reduce anxiety*)
5 D (*people feel that … consuming one or two of these products, they can reap all the benefits*)
6 C (*boosts mental development*)
7 B (*sales of healthy or lifestyle foods are worth over £1 billion*)

MODULE 3
3.1
Starting a business

1
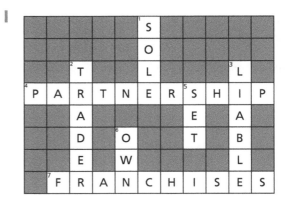

2　1 F　2 D　3 B　4 C　5 A

3　1 growth　2 profit　3 enthusiastic　4 tested
5 sense　6 hard　7 fail　8 risks　9 capital　10 run

4
1 Present simple
2 *going to*
3 Future perfect
4 *will* (promise)
5 *will* (prediction)
6 Present continuous

5
1 **By the end of the year we** will have sold over one million units.
2 **This time tomorrow I** will be lying on a beach in Bermuda. I can't wait!
3 I'm meeting her **in the pub at 6 o'clock.**
4 The seminar takes place **at 11am, followed by lunch at 1pm.**
5 **I think that she** will probably get the job.
6 **I've decided that I** am going to set up my own consultancy business.

6
1 'm having
2 'll be driving
3 'm going to tell
4 leaves, will get
5 will win, will try
6 will have finished
7 'll help
8 'm going to play, 'll be relaxing

3.2
Leaving and taking messages

1
1 the fourteenth of May two thousand and nine
2 two to five pee em
3 Oh-double seven-eight, three-two-two, one-oh-one-oh OR one-zero-one-zero
4 Jay-gee-one-three-ex
5 Oh-apostrophe-are-ee-ay-double ell-why
6 Double you double you double you dot yell dot com
7 Karen at gmail dot eff are

2 1 hold   2 returning   3 read   4 back   5 get   6 reason

3 A 6   B 5   C 0   D 1   E 3   F 2   G 4

4 1 to   2 out   3 regard   4 by   5 back   6 grateful
7 call   8 on   9 read   10 for

5
Message for: Mico Jurevic
From: Jose Moya
Subject: Mr Moya picked up your diary by mistake yesterday.
Action needed: Call Mr Moya back in the office today or on his mobile.
Contact details: Mobile number 06966 39941

6
A
Message for: Ms Gerhard
Message from: **Aran** at **Bangkok House Restaurant**
Subject: He has **prepared menu** and **price** for set dinner.
Action: Please call him **on 0208 733 4545.**

B
Message for: Mr Sato
Message from: **John Davies**
Subject: **Confidential**
Action: Please **call him** as soon as possible.

C
Message from: Terry Jones
Subject: Please note that the **offer** on **office chairs** ends **this week**.
Action: Let **him know** soon if we are interested.

D
Message for: Sarah Jenas
Message from: **Maria Sanchez**
Subject: She apologised for **missing** the **appointment on** Friday. Would like to **change to** Thursday afternoon.
Action: Please call to **confirm**.

7

/eɪ/	/iː/	/aɪ/	/əʊ/	/ɑː/	/uː/	/e/
A	E	I	O	R	Q	Z
H	G	Y			U	
J	T				W	

8 1 Jagger   2 Stipe   3 Cobain

3.3
Listening Test: Part One

2
A
Changes to conference
Date: (**1**) **3 May**
Venue: (**2**) **National Institute**
3–4pm session: Speaker cancelled
New speaker: (**3**) **Steve Johnson**
Title: (**4**) **Mobile Future**

B

Customer Services – Messages
Caller's name: Jackie Brown
Company: **(5) Global Media** Limited
Item Ordered: **(6) Leather sofa**
Problem: Incorrect invoice. We **(7) overcharged** the customer.
Action: Credit **(8) £300** to her account.

C

Reminder of Training Session:
Date: 4 July
Course Title: **(9) Buying signals**
Participants: **(10) Sales managers**
Venue: Galaxy Hotel
To reserve a place: Send back **(11) registration form** to Lisa Melrose in HR.

D

HR department – Messages
Caller's name: Buddy Richards
Subject: Job interview
Problem: He has an interview on **(12) 10 July** but he is unable to attend because he is **(13) on holiday**. He is very **(14) interested in** the job. Is it possible for us to give him a **(15) telephone interview**?

MODULE 4

4.1
Advertising

1 1 word of mouth 2 loyalty card 3 billboard 4 spam
5 mailshot 6 sample 7 banner 8 TV commercial

2 1 to 2 about 3 for 4 to 5 to 6 to 7 at 8 at

3 1 B 2 A 3 E 4 D

4 1 suppose 2 not sure 3 On the other hand
4 relatively 5 Remember

5 1 mustn't 2 don't have to 3 mustn't 4 don't have to
5 must 6 should

6 1 can't have 2 must have 3 must 4 can't have
5 can't 6 must

7 1 AIDS
2 No (*changes will have to be made*)
3 Yes (*we had already improved it*)
4 They chose not to make the advert 'more pleasant to look at'.

8 1 They should have / ought to have used an advertising agency.
2 They should have / ought to have used a different type of advertising.
3 They should / ought to advertise in the local paper.
4 They should / ought to introduce a loyalty card.
5 He should have / ought to have installed an anti-virus programme.

4.2
Delegating

1 1 E Time to accept change
2 A Growing into new roles
3 B Don't be afraid to bring in expertise
4 D Planning for the future

2 1 priority 2 brief 3 free 4 ensure 5 updates
6 through 7 deadline 8 charge

3 1 Please give priority to the Johnson case.
2 Let me know your answer by Tuesday.
3 You've done a great job on this!
4 One thing that's worrying me is the cost.
5 Can I borrow your computer for a moment?
6 I want you to go to Geneva.
7 When is the deadline for registration?
8 The main findings of the report were positive.

5 1 A 2 F 3 B 4 G 5 C 6 D

6 1 B 2 D 3 A 4 C 5 G 6 F

7 **Suggested answer:**
To: The executive board
Re: Results of recent advertising campaigns

Introduction and aims
This report sets out to examine the results of recent advertising campaigns on sales figures, and to suggest how we can improve our advertising strategy.

Findings: Effect of advertising on sales
In late February we mailed out a special offers catalogue to all our customers. This had positive results and sales in March increased by 35 per cent. In June we carried out a short TV advertising campaign, which was expensive and achieved a very poor response. As you can see from the chart, sales continued to fall following this campaign. In September, we launched a series of newspaper adverts which were more successful, although they were also quite expensive. Finally, in November we mailed out our new catalogue. Sales continued to increase slightly following this mailout.

Conclusions

The most successful advertising was the mailout of the special offers catalogue. The other campaigns achieved disappointing results.

Recommendations

We would recommend mailing out a special offers catalogue again. We would not recommend TV and newspaper advertising due to the high costs and poor results. We would also suggest investigating new possibilities, such as Internet advertising.

4.3

Writing Test: Part One

1 Suggested answer:

Following the changes in the tax law announced last week, the rate of social security tax will increase from 10 per cent to 11 per cent from July. This new rate will apply to all employees. For further information please contact me in the HR department between 9am and 5pm.

Reading Test: Part Five

2 1 For most people, it is more better to have an interesting job than a high salary. (*Comparative form 'better' does not require 'more'.*)

2 The company encourages a people to go on training courses. (*'a' cannot be used with a plural noun.*)

3 It is a job with a lot of variety and which with flexible working hours. (*'which' is used to introduce a relative clause.*)

4 When you join to the company, you become part of a family. (*'join' does not require a preposition.*)

5 But it is not only the company's responsibility. Each employee that has to motivate himself. (*'that' is used to introduce a clause.*)

3 1 AT
2 IF
3 TO
4 LIKE
5 CORRECT
6 MAKES
7 YOU
8 CORRECT

MODULE 5

5.1

The workplace

1 1 What kind of art do companies tend to buy?
2 How does a company ever agree on what art to buy?
3 Why do so many companies choose to buy art?
4 Who should I consult if I want to buy a piece of art?

5 Does it matter where the art is displayed?
6 Can you commission a work of art to emphasise your brand?

2 1 aims   2 end   3 commissioned   4 manager
5 scope   6 much   7 spend   8 specialist   9 cope
10 oversee   11 requirements   12 on   13 within
14 checking

3 1 worldwide   2 requirements   3 referrals
4 satisfaction   5 expertise   6 combination
7 outcome   8 appointment

4 1 In words ending in *-tion* or *-sion* we usually stress the syllable before this ending.
2 combi**na**tion   di**vi**sion   so**lu**tion   instal**la**tion
4 de**vel**opment   a**gree**ment   enter**tain**ment   re**quire**ment   ap**poin**tment   in**vest**ment
5 When the suffix *-ment* is added to a verb to make a noun, the stress remains on the same syllable.

5

Direct speech	Reported speech
I **am** too old	was
I **don't know**	**didn't know**
I **haven't seen** him	**hadn't seen**
You **have to** apply	**had to**
I **can** manage	**could**
It**'s raining** here	**was raining**
I **live** in Paris	**lived**
I **was waiting** for an hour	**had been waiting**
I **won't** tell anyone	**wouldn't tell**
I **can't** understand	**couldn't understand**

6 1 Works of art and artistic events.
2 They must be for public display.
3 It will give a boost to the arts in Britain.

7 1 A spokesperson for Harris Plumbing said that it wouldn't really affect them, as they did not sponsor any art projects anyway.
2 A spokesperson for Riverside Centre said that they were not against it, but they wished they would do the same for sports sponsorship.
3 A spokesperson for Max's Café said that it was right for the government to reduce taxes on companies, but they had to decide where they could spend their money.
4 A spokesperson for Jones Gallery said that it was about time. They said that this government had a bad record on promoting the arts.
5 A spokesperson for The Bus Company said that they thought it was a really good idea. It would help to bring art closer to the people.

6 A spokesperson for Ashton Community Centre said that they hoped this would give employees a chance to show their artistic talents.

7 A spokesperson for Opera Now said that it was not clear whether this also applied to musical performances, but they hoped so.

8 A spokesperson for Telecom asked if it was really true.

8 'We apologise for the inconvenience to passengers following the closure of the York to Newcastle line. This is due to an accident involving two freight trains. Fortunately, no-one has been injured. The line will reopen on Tuesday morning after we have made repairs. In the meantime, passengers are asked to use other means of transport.'

5.2
Participating in a meeting

1 1 Chairperson   2 minutes   3 attend   4 agenda
5 informal   6 holding   7 reach   8 point
9 along   10 on

2 1 reached an   2 It seems to me   3 I agree
4 I suggest that we / I'd like to suggest that we
5 I disagree with you there   6 come in

3 1 He uses them to warn people if they say something rude.
2 He schedules the meeting early to give people time to relax before the meeting actually starts.
3 It helps people to concentrate.
4 People can give their opinion more openly.
5 He cancels a meeting and asks people to use the time to look for ideas.

4 1 CORRECT
2 THE
3 OF
4 DO
5 CORRECT
6 MORE
7 ARE
8 WHICH
9 IF
10 CORRECT
11 THE
12 HAVE
13 TO
14 CORRECT

5 **Suggested answer:**
Subject: Art commission
This report describes the decisions taken on commissioning an artwork for the reception area of the new company offices. The main points agreed are as follows:

- A sculpture will be the best type of artwork for the space. The work is expected to cost around £10,000, but the maximum budget is £20,000.
- We will employ an art consultant for half a day to get advice on how to manage the project (Diego Sanchez will find the right consultant).
- Michiko Makio will make a list of possible artists and present it at the next meeting.
- The artist chosen will make the final decision on the exact character of the sculpture, but will be given some ideas to work from. These suggestions will be presented at the next meeting, to be held on 2 August.

5.3
Speaking Test: Part Two

1 1 F   2 T   3 T   4 F   5 T   6 F

2 **Good points:**
Includes introduction, main body and conclusion.
Separates points using *first, second, third.*
Gives specific example for delivery time.
Invites comments from partner.

Bad points:
Doesn't give specific information about first two points, price and quality.

3 1 **In** my view
2 The second~~ly~~ is the quality
3 the third is the ~~period of~~ delivery **time**
4 the time it **takes** from
5 the delivery ~~into~~ the factory
6 In some industries, this ~~must be~~ **is** a
7 I think **it** is very difficult
8 who will ~~can~~ meet all of these conditions
9 the price will ~~be also~~ **also be** high

4 1 First of **all** ...
2 The second point to **consider** is that ...
3 It is also true **that** many companies ...
4 Something **else** that is important is ...
5 **For** example, if you need to ...
6 **In** conclusion, I think ...

MODULE 6
6.1
Recruitment

1 1 D   2 C   3 C   4 B   5 A   6 D   7 C   8 D   9 B
10 B   11 A   12 C

2 1 G   2 E   3 C   4 A   5 H   6 I   7 D   8 B

3
1 dismissed (*You are made redundant when your job is no longer needed. You are usually dismissed when a company is not happy with your work.*)
2 retire (*You retire from a company when you stop working, usually at around 65. You resign from a company to work somewhere else.*)
3 recruit (*You recruit someone when you get them to join the company. You hire someone when you pay them to do a job.*)
4 leave (*You usually leave a company to take another job or do something else, and you receive no extra pay. When you take voluntary redundancy you receive redundancy pay to compensate you for losing your job.*)

4
1 fine   2 stayed   3 look   4 fork   5 tyre

5
1 car park   2 laboratory   3 reception   4 lift
5 staff room / staff noticeboard

6
1 All members are invited to attend a union meeting on Friday 12 July.
2 Anything suspicious should be reported to security immediately.
3 Suggestions can be posted in this box.
4 This building was opened by Queen Elizabeth in 1988.
5 A registration form must be obtained from the Administration Office.

7
1 Holbroke has been sacked by capital investors.
2 400 jobs will be created in the North West.
3 The CEO has resigned after record losses were announced at Teleast.
4 Temporary workers were given only 1 day's notice.
5 A report shows that 300 new doctors are needed.
6 The England football manager has resigned.

8
1 It's better to be respected than to be liked.
2 I dislike being told what to do.
3 It's nice to be considered for a promotion.
4 I don't like to be kept waiting.
5 I don't mind my decisions being questioned.

6.2
Electronic communication

1
1 C   2 B   3 E   4 G   5 D

2
1 deleted   2 resend   3 forgot   4 know   5 work
6 check   7 received   8 access   9 key   10 click

3
1 E   2 A   3 D   4 I   5 H   6 C   7 G   8 J   9 F

4
Suggested answer:
Dear Liane
Thank you for sending me your presentation. I have looked through it and generally it looks good. Unfortunately, it also contains a few factual mistakes. Perhaps we could meet some time to go through it and discuss these. Let me know a time that suits you.

5
1 remind   2 please   3 appreciate   4 regard   5 reason
6 grateful   7 suggestions   8 note

6.3
Reading Test: Part Two

1 **Suggested answers:**
1 One is to advertise the job in the newspaper.
2 Do you enjoy your job?
3 I think the design has serious weaknesses.
4 The second was a great improvement.
5 77 per cent were very unhappy.
6 Nowadays, it is unusual to stay in the same job for more than ten years.

2   1 A   2 D   3 C   4 B   5 F

MODULE 7
7.1
Job qualities

1
1 sales pitch   2 door-to-door selling   3 target-driven
4 tangible results   5 sales techniques

2

Positive	Negative
rewarding, dynamic, well-paid, challenging, tangible, sociable	dishonest, unglamorous, unpopular, repetitive

3
1 rewarding   2 frustrating   3 repetitive   4 variety
5 interesting   6 boredom   7 responsibility
8 well-paid

4   de**b**t   autum**n**   enviro**n**ment   **w**hole   busi**n**ess
mortgage   **k**nowledge   **g**uard   **h**our   **w**rong   lis**t**en
b**u**ilding   dou**b**t   clim**b**

5

Adjective (or adverb)	Comparative form	Superlative form
high	higher	the highest
low	lower	the lowest
good	better	the best
well (adverb)	better	the best
bad	worse	the worst
flexible	more flexible	the most flexible
rich	richer	the richest
far	further	the furthest
pretty	prettier	the prettiest
boring	more boring	the most boring
little	less	the least
much	more	the most

6 1 The   2 than   3 more   4 as   5 even   6 better
7 most   8 worse

7 1 ~~than~~ **as** me
2 the ~~reliablest~~ **most reliable**
3 the ~~better~~ **best** price
4 my ~~nearer~~ **nearest**
5 a ~~more close~~ **closer** look
6 so ~~more~~ **many** people
7 ~~highest~~ **higher** than
8 just as ~~cheaper~~ **cheap**
9 similar prices ~~with~~ **to**
10 ~~many~~ **much** higher

7.2
Selling

1

F	A	I	L		K	N	O	W	S
	B			R		O			T
	L			E			I		U
B	E	N	E	F	I	T	S		F
U		E		L			S		F
I		E		E		B	U	Y	
L		D		C			E		
D		S		T	R	U	S	T	

2 1 in, mind   2 come, updated   3 prove, on   4 about, put
5 much, give   6 wondering, with

3 1 understand / respond to / establish / meet
2 close / make   3 compare / sell   4 make / receive
5 explain / emphasise / stress

4 1 B   2 E   3 D   4 A   5 H   6 C   7 G

5 1 They are central and convenient for clients.
2 The offices are too small and poorly equipped, and more business is coming from outside the city.
3 More office space, a more modern building and more car parking.
4 He wants to know the fees.

6 **Suggested answer:**
Dear Mr Smith
Thank you for **your letter concerning new offices**.
We would be delighted **to help you find more convenient premises for your company**.
At the moment we have two suitable **properties for rent**.
One is **the first floor (1,400 m²) of a new office block in the Milton Industrial Park**. Its key features are:
- **good access to main roads**
- **flexible working space**
- **modern fittings (lights, computer cables etc)**
- **parking for 12 cars**
The other is an attractive **office building on the outskirts of the city (1,000 m²)**. Its advantages are that:
- **it has good public transport links**
- **it is located near a public park**
- **it has a low rent**
Full details of our fees can be **found on our website**.
Please do not hesitate **to contact me for further details**.
I look forward **to hearing from you**.

7.3
Reading Test: Part Four

1 1 C   2 D   3 A   4 C   5 C

2 1 A   2 C   3 D   4 B   5 B   6 D   7 D   8 C   9 A
10 B   11 B   12 D

MODULE 8
8.1
Training

1 1 C   2 C   3 D   4 A   5 B   6 D   7 A   8 C   9 B
10 D

2

Advantage	Disadvantage
a plus	the downside
one good thing	one drawback
a benefit	one problem
a positive point	one thing against

3 1 ↘↗   2 ↘   3 ↗   4 ↘   5 ↗   6 ↘↗   7 ↘
8 ↘↗   9 ↗   10 ↘

4

-ing form	+ Infinitive (to do)	Both possible
involve	afford	remember
recommend	want	stop
be interested in	would like	like
		start
		prefer

5 1 to speak, to call   2 seeing, calling
3 switching, restarting   4 using   5 to risk   6 attending
7 to come

7 online, by correspondence, in a group, one to one

8.2
Showing you're listening

1 1 A   2 B   3 B

2 1 +   2 +   3 +   4 –   5 –   6 +   7 +   8 –   9 –

3 + phrases often ask questions; they focus on what the other person is thinking or saying.
– phrases often include the word *I* or *me* and focus on the speaker's feelings, opinions or experiences.

4 1 do   2 with   3 putting   4 as   5 ~~of~~   6 would
7 I know   8 recruit   9 them questions   10 That
11 more   12 doing

5 1 E   2 F   3 C   4 B   5 A

6 1 In addition to being a very effective training course, it can be done in only two days.
2 Because of bad weather, the session was cancelled.
3 Despite only six people enrolling on the course, it went ahead anyway.
4 Following a discussion on the issue, we took a vote.

7 1 As a result   2 Unfortunately   3 despite   4 However
5 Moreover   6 In addition to   7 due to   8 Nevertheless

8.3
Listening Test: Part Two

1 1 H   2 E   3 A   4 C   5 F

2 6 G   7 C   8 H   9 A   10 F

MODULE 9
9.1
Branding

1 1 brand identity
2 advertising slogan
3 big impact
4 customer perception
5 attractive packaging
6 marketing tool

2 1 quality
2 local
3 ultimate

3 1 BMW
2 Levi's
3 HSBC

4 0 A (*a responsibility to be sensitive to other cultures*)
1 D (*The world still wants American products, but not necessarily an American lifestyle.*)
2 C (*they change their products so that they suit local tastes*)
3 A (*Americans have a poor record of going abroad to research foreign markets*)
4 C (*they try to … build trust with local consumers*)
5 B (*other policies made the USA less popular internationally*)
6 D (*more international marketing case studies are being used*)

5 1 which   2 whose   3 when   4 why   5 who
6 where   7 which   8 which

6 1 Necessary
2 Omitted: It is the first new product we have launched in six years.
3 Necessary
4 Necessary
5 Necessary
6 Omitted: The company we used last year has gone out of business.
7 Necessary
8 Omitted: He's a man I respect very much.

7 **Suggested answers:**
1 New York is the kind of place *where anything can happen.*
2 Your 20's are a period in your life *when you find your direction.*
3 My parents are the reason *why I became a doctor.*
4 It's the kind of book *which you can't put down.*
5 The iPhone is the kind of product *which changes everyone's way of life.*
6 He's the kind of manager *who people respect.*

9.2
Getting through

1   1 D   2 F   3 G   4 E   5 A   6 C

2   **Suggested answers:**
1 I'll look it up.
2 I'll read that back to you.
3 I'm tied up at the moment.
4 We've run out of time, I'm afraid.
5 I'll try to bring it forward to Thursday.
6 I'll call back later.
7 I'll put you through.
8 I'll pass the message on to her.

3   1 connect   2 in   3 take   4 put
    5 take   6 moment   7 hold   8 calling
    9 back   10 convenient   11 suits   12 pass

4   Dear Rebecca
I am **still** waiting **for** an answer to the email I sent you last week. My colleague Erica **needs** to know your answer before she **goes** to Germany. Please let **me** know by W**ednes**day at the latest.
Thanks
Jane

Hello John
I **tried** to telephone you yesterday, but I think you were out at ~~the~~ lunch with a client. We are having a meeting **tomorrow** at 10 o'clock with a brand consultant to discuss ~~about~~ our new marketing campaign. He is a very in**teres**ting guy who **has** worked with some top companies, so please try to come.
Felix

Dear Mr Duncan
Regarding ~~to~~ your order for a Bosch washing machine, I am afraid that this item **is** not in stock. However, I can offer you **an**other option, which is a German-made machine, **too**. I **have attached** a full description of the product to this email and I hope it will meet your r**equirem**ents.
Yours sincerely
Onkar (Sales)

Dear Maria
I got your message ~~in~~ this morning about the interviews which will take place **next week**. In ~~the~~ answer to your question, I think it **would** be better if they were group interviews. This will give us the **oppor**tunity to see how the different candidates **interact** with each other.
Thanks
Jane

9.3
Writing Test: Part Two

1   A   The student didn't cover all the points. The following were not mentioned:
- that the price of cars can vary between locations
- drop off times
- that for Newcastle they would need to use a partner firm, Geordie Car Rental.

D   The style is a little too conversational; *Thanks, What's more, it'd be good to know, give me a call, a good time to meet*

2   **Suggested answer:**
Dear Mr Duffy
Thank you very much for choosing our company. We **would be very pleased** to have the chance to work with you. **Moreover**, if you **would consider extending** the trial period to 12 months, we could offer you another 8 per cent reduction in the price.
Here are the answers to your other points:
– Our normal collection hours are 7am–8pm. There **is** a small fee for collection at other times. **Cars may be dropped off at any time**.
– We can cover all the locations mentioned, but it **would** be good to know how many cars you expect to hire from each place. **(In Newcastle we would be working with a partner firm, who are very reliable.)**
– We can also **provide** chauffeur driven cars.
– **The prices of our cars vary a little from one location to another, but this is something we can discuss.**
All in all, I think you can be confident that we **will** handle this business professionally and **at a competitive** price.
Please **contact me to arrange a convenient** time to meet.
Yours sincerely
Steve **Johns**

MODULE 10

10.1
Management

1   1 Develop   2 Recognise, fill
    3 Plan, implement   4 Renew

2   1 fail   2 weaknesses   3 success
    4 aware   5 rapidly   6 learn

3   1 rapidly   2 strategy   3 recognise   4 awareness
    5 success   6 weak   7 set   8 implementation

4
1. CAN
2. CORRECT
3. SO
4. CORRECT
5. THAN
6. ABOUT
7. AN
8. BEEN
9. TO
10. CORRECT

5
1. Correct
2. Incorrect: will never achieve
3. Incorrect: heat
4. Correct
5. Incorrect: hadn't met
6. Incorrect: have
7. Incorrect: were
8. Correct
9. Incorrect: keeps
10. Incorrect: failed

6 1 C 2 F 3 H 4 G 5 B 6 D 7 A

7 Suggested answers:
1. He wouldn't have developed his singing if he hadn't joined a choir.
2. He wouldn't have started to record his own songs if he hadn't left the music school.
3. If he hadn't gone to Los Angeles, he wouldn't have met the actor Jamie Foxx.
4. If he hadn't supported Taylor Swift, he wouldn't have achieved greater fame.

10.2
Solving problems

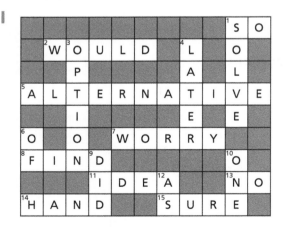

2
1. could / might   2 find   3 person's   4 are
5. were   6 a good   7 of   8 few
9. would   10 by   11 to write
12. do   13 so   14 well

3
1. ahead   2 in   3 within
4. over   5 out   6 behind

4 1 B 2 D 3 A 4 C

5
1. Following / Further to
2. In order to
3. Therefore / So

6
1. Because of the high demand for the training course next week, we have decided to move it to a larger venue. The course will now take place at the Marriot Hotel on 4 March.
2. Unfortunately, we have experienced a few problems with the new software. This is due to a programming fault. We are trying to correct it and, with luck, it will be working again by tomorrow afternoon at the latest.
3. Further to our meeting last week, I have been working on a proposal for our new Chinese partner. However, it will not be ready in time for our next meeting. I am attaching it to this email. Could you look at it and tell me how it can be improved?
4. I am still waiting for a response to my request of 12 September concerning purchases of office stationery. I need this information in order to prepare the budgets for next year.
   Please send the information as soon as possible. I am running out of time.

10.3
Listening Test: Part Three

1
1. B a big mystery.
2. A include all the things that you have to do.
3. A leave until another day.
4. B use the time to do some personal jobs.
5. B feel tired.
6. B agree to any deadlines.
7. C get home earlier at the end of the day.
8. A wastes the company's time.

2 1 A 2 B 3 C 4 C 5 C 6 A 7 B 8 C

MODULE 11

11.1
Ethical economics

1
1 GDP   2 break-even   3 overheads
4 freight   5 markup   6 a commodity
7 export costs   8 market price

2 export   insurance   staffing   maintenance   additional

3
1 paid   2 exported   3 transported
4 bought   5 packaged   6 sold

4
1 average   2 tiny   3 small   4 increasing
5 excessive   6 minimum   7 least

5
1 **a** taxi
2 **some** information
3 **the** biggest
4 **The** train
5 **an** enormous increase
6 at ~~the~~ work.
7 in **the** Red Lion
8 **a** very bad
9 **the** last five years
10 **some** paper

6
1 I work at (**0**) night and sleep in **the** day.
2 We are based in (**0**) Germany but we operate all over **the** world.
3 In **the** last ten years, we have taken on (**0**) 40 new employees.
4 **The** United Nations was founded in 1945 after **the** Second World War.
5 I need to be at (**0**) home in time for (**0**) supper.
6 Will you go to (**0**) university next year?
7 My son is studying at **the** University of California.

7 vulnerable   comfortable   medicine   secretary   ordinary
difference   interested   business   valuable   withdrawal

8
1 few
2 a
3 on
4 to
5 ~~about~~
6 past ten
7 must ~~to~~
8 necessarily
9 to operate
10 make
11 Meeting, seeing

11.2
Discussing trends

1
1 decrease   2 fall   3 soar
4 peak   5 remain stable

2
1 fall   2 increase   3 level out   4 remain

3
1 B   2 B   3 C   4 B   5 C   6 D   7 B   8 C   9 C
10 A

4
1 G   2 B   3 H   4 A   5 F   6 D   7 E

5   **Introducing a proposal**
We would be delighted to work with you
Before I give more details I would like to point out that …
The main elements of our proposal are as follows:
Comparing pros and cons
The advantage of using a hotel would be …
One other thing we should consider is …
Balancing and concluding
In order to keep the overall cost down I would recommend that …
Please don't hesitate to contact me if you would like to discuss any of these points

6   **Suggested answer:**
Dear Mr Cook
Thank you for your letter regarding an evening event for your staff and customers. We would be delighted to work with you. Before I give more details, I would like to point out that we have over ten years' experience in organising successful events for large companies.
The main elements of our proposal are as follows:
- The venue we suggest is the Churchill Hotel Banquet Hall. The advantage of using a hotel would be that any guests who need to stay over for the night can stay in the hotel.
- The well-known comedian, Jo Bland, will do a half-hour session at the end of the dinner. After that, a live band will supply the music for dancing.

One other thing we should consider is whether you or one of your staff will want to give a speech and if so what equipment is needed.
As to the cost, I expect the figure to be around £40 per head. In order to keep the overall cost down, I would recommend that guests pay for their drinks at the bar.
Please don't hesitate to contact me if you would like to discuss any of these points. I look forward to hearing from you.
Yours sincerely

11.3
Reading Test: Part Three

1 1 B 2 C 3 D 4 A 5 A 6 C

MODULE 12
12.1
Business law

1 **sue** someone
take **legal** action against someone
take out **litigation** against someone
start legal **proceedings** against someone
prosecute someone for

2
1 court
2 copyright
3 prosecute (sue)
4 defence
5 trademark
6 rights
7 case
8 sue (prosecute)
9 compensation
10 litigation

3 1 C 2 F 3 B 4 E 5 G 6 A

4
1 You're French, aren't you?
2 Do you think they are going to sue?
3 Do you know what this is about ?
4 I was wondering if you could help me?
5 Do you know when I have to register?
6 Can you tell me who is in charge?
7 I'd like to know why she left.
8 You're open to new offers, aren't you?
9 Can you explain how it works?
10 I'd like to know how long you have worked here.

5
1 I'd like to know what you think.
2 Could you tell me how much it costs?
3 Do you think it is legal?
4 I was wondering how long it would take.
5 Can you tell me exactly what they complained about?
6 I wonder if they own the rights to the name?
7 Do you remember which firm you used?

6
1 We met at the Berlin conference, didn't we?
2 Li is your first name, isn't it?
3 The meeting has been postponed, hasn't it?
4 You take sugar in your coffee, don't you?
5 I'm not late, am I?
6 They own the rights to the name, don't they?
7 He works for ABC, doesn't he?

7 /iː/
legal, recent, secret, previous, detail, retail, medium, female
/e/
level, metal, precious, separate, decade, creditor, pressure

12.2
Handling questions

1
1 follow
2 answer
3 come back
4 mean
5 get back
6 mind
7 repeat
8 Thank
9 catch
10 is

2
1 Sorry, I didn't catch that. OR Can you repeat the question?
2 Let me get back to you on that.
3 That's a good question.
4 I'll come back to that point later on.
5 Sorry, I don't follow you. OR Sorry, can you explain what you mean exactly?

3 1 A 2 C 3 B 4 D

4
1 made
2 a
3 before / by
4 ~~of~~
5 has been
6 using
7 nothing
8 ~~more~~
9 these
10 as
11 to expand
12 to
13 from

5 Press release C: It is written in the first person, (*We are pleased ...*); it doesn't contain information of general or public interest. In other words, it's more like an advertisement than a press release.

6 **Suggested answer:**

The contract to build a new tram line linking the centre of Liverpool to the Birkenhead area has been won by Sestro. The total value of the contract is £16.5 million, but part of this sum will be put towards the building of a community youth centre and skateboard park. A spokesman from Liverpool City Council said that he was very happy that the project would not only benefit travellers in and out of Liverpool city centre but also young people in the area. Work is due to begin in January next year.

7 <u>fu</u>ture oppor<u>tu</u>nity pro<u>du</u>ce <u>mu</u>sic va<u>lue</u> <u>due</u> un<u>u</u>sual

12.3

Speaking Test: Part Three

1 Candidate A's answers are too long and formal.
Candidate B's answers are too short and sound rude.

2 1 E 2 I 3 G 4 J 5 A 6 B 7 H 8 F 9 C

3
1 discount
2 the other
3 effective
4 like / such as
5 save
6 commute / come
7 interested
8 do